FRESH SPANISH

SERGIO VASQUEZ

METRO BOOKS
NEW YORK

To Delia Tartera Coll and Nuria Martinez Tartera, with thanks for all their help in this project.

Note

Ovens should be preheated to the specified temperature—if using a fan-assisted oven, follow the manufacturer's instructions for adjusting the time and the temperature.

Fresh herbs should be used unless otherwise stated.

Medium eggs should be used unless otherwise stated.

The Food and Drug Administration advises that eggs should not be consumed raw. This book contains some dishes made with raw or lightly cooked eggs. It is prudent for vulnerable people such as pregnant and nursing mothers, invalids, the elderly, babies, and young children to avoid uncooked or lightly cooked dishes made with eggs. Once prepared, these dishes should be kept refrigerated and used promptly.

This book includes dishes made with nuts and nut derivatives. It is advisable for those with known allergic reactions to nuts and nut derivatives and those who may be potentially vulnerable to these allergies, such as pregnant and nursing mothers, invalids, the elderly, babies, and children, to avoid dishes made with nuts and nut oils. It is also prudent to check the labels of pre-prepared ingredients for the possible inclusion of nut derivatives.

Contents

Introduction

Spanish cooking enjoys the full benefit of the vibrant natural flavors and health-promoting properties for which the Mediterranean diet is famed. Spain's cuisine is based on an abundant supply of quality local produce—from luscious sun-ripened tomatoes and sweet peppers to juicy oranges, peaches, and figs; from expertly produced meats and freshly hauled fish to an impressive array of cheeses. The cooking is characterized by a unique, distinctive mix of flavors, enriched by complex historical influences as well as special techniques and a particular approach to eating. This book taps into the best that Spanish cuisine has to offer, celebrating its approach to food as a laid-back, joyful, and healthy way of life.

Spanish cuisine is rich with the country's history, displaying the influences of a varied past. The Moors from North Africa, who spent some 800 years in Spain, brought with them their favorite foods and flavorings such as almonds, eggplants, cinnamon, cumin, nutmeg, and honey, as well as culinary techniques such as cooking meat on skewers over an open fire, frying in olive oil, and preserving in vinegar. The Spanish words for rice, *arroz*, oil, *aceite*, and almonds, *almendras*, are all Arabic in origin.

The Jewish community, which settled in Spain over several centuries, also left its mark on various classic Spanish dishes. Not least of these is *cocido (see page 105)*, Spain's national dish of slow-simmered meat, vegetables, and chickpeas, which closely resembles *dafina*, the Sabbath stew of the Sephardi Jews.

Catholicism, too, has had a significant influence on Spanish cuisine. Salt cod, which plays such a key role in Spanish cooking, was preserved for fast days, and pork became an integral part of the cuisine simply because it had been forbidden by both the Moors and Jews who were subsequently ejected from the country. During the time of the Spanish Inquisition, eating pork became a proof of loyalty to the Catholic Church.

Added to these religious influences, there are of course regional influences in Spanish cooking, with the plains, mountains, and sea offering a wonderful variety of produce. Each region makes the most of its natural wealth, giving a unique character to the cuisine of that area. Along the Pyrenees lie the Basque country, Navarre, and Aragon, each with its own distinctive cooking. In the Basque country you will find fabulous seafood from both the Mediterranean and Atlantic—and salt cod is big business. From Navarre comes a bounty of wonderful vegetables and from Aragon's mountains a wealth of game. In the north, Galicia is frequently referred to as the seafood province, while Asturias is known for its hearty bean and sausage dishes, including the famous *fabada*, as well as its superior cheeses.

In central Spain—Madrid, northern Castile and Leon, New Castile, La Mancha, and Extremadura—you will find food with strong, robust flavors, with roast pork and lamb, slow-simmered stews, and flavorful vegetable dishes being common fare. Extremadura is particularly well known for its premium pigs and of course the resulting hams, sausages, and pâtés.

Andalusia in the south exhibits a noticeable Arab influence in its cuisine, as does its architecture, agriculture, music, and gardening. Its most famous foods are its green olives and red dried hams, but fish and seafood are also a draw. The area has a thriving agriculture, growing a rich variety of fruit and vegetables.

Catalonia and Levante lie along the east coast. The Catalan cuisine reveals certain French influences, and serves up wonderful fish and seafood dishes. Rustic meals using beans and sausages are popular, too. Levante is home to Valencia, the birthplace of what may be Spain's most famous dish, paella—but there are also many other wonderful rice dishes to sample. Together, the regions of Spain offer perhaps the most varied array of nourishing and delicious dishes to be found in any one national cuisine.

Eating Spanish style

Spanish life revolves around food, beginning with breakfast eaten in a bar on the way to work, followed by a long, leisurely lunch consumed around 2 pm, then a snack after work, and ending with a supper late in the evening. Meals are seen as a time for coming together and socializing, but it is not just full-blown meals that offer the opportunity for social interaction. Tapas—that most valued of Spanish inventions—is the perfect way to get together informally with friends and catch up over a drink and a light bite. It all began in Andalusia, and the legend goes that a slice of bread topped with bread or cheese was placed over a glass to keep off the flies (the Spanish word *tapa* means "cover.") The tradition spread and you will find tapas bars all over Spain, filled with people chatting, drinking, and eating. Like all Spanish food, tapas make the most of fresh local ingredients and vary according to season and region. The tapas themselves range from the lightest nibbles, such as marinated olives *(see page 41)*, to more substantial snacks such as the classic potato and tomato dish, *patatas bravas (see page 48)*, and meatballs *(albóndigas)* in a spiced tomato sauce *(see page 22)*.

Fiestas and celebrations, too, are a time for eating and drinking. There are special foods for feast days, and every town has its own fiesta in which people gather to celebrate, eat, and drink. Literally thousands of these fiestas take place across the country in a single year.

HEALTHY EATING While the variety, freshness, and quality of the ingredients used in Spanish cooking naturally create a nutritious and well-balanced diet, all the recipes in this book have been specially selected and crafted with health in mind. For example, unsaturated fats have been chosen in preference to saturated ones. Unsaturated fats, such as the olive oil that plays such an important role in Spanish cuisine, help to increase the ratio of "good" cholesterol (which is carried in the blood by high-density lipoproteins or HDL) to "bad" cholesterol (which is carried in the blood by the low-density lipoproteins or LDL). In contrast, saturated fats, such as butter, increase the blood's quantity of "bad" LDL cholesterol, associated with increased risk of cardiovascular disease.

It's well known that eating too much salt can raise blood pressure, potentially leading to heart disease and stroke. Fortunately, Spanish cooking is rich in delicious, healthy flavorings, such as fresh Mediterranean herbs, spices, and aromatics. The amount of added salt in the recipes has been reduced in favor of sprinklings of fresh herbs such as parsley, tarragon, and mint, spices such as *pimentón*, cinnamon, and saffron, and healthy flavorings such as garlic and lemon juice.

The generous use of fresh, seasonal vegetables is one of the joys of the Spanish table, as well as one of the reasons why the cuisine is so good for you. These recipes feature a wide range of fresh vegetables, incorporating them both raw and cooked to make the most of their fabulous colors, flavors, and textures. Also liberally included in the recipes is fresh fruit, which the Spanish climate produces in such glorious abundance. In Spain, fruit is used in both sweet and savory dishes—oranges, for example, which are a brilliant source of vitamin C, are frequently cooked with chicken and fish, and are also often used in desserts *(see pages 104 and 152)*.

For the meat and poultry recipes, it is the low-fat cuts that have been chosen. There are also plenty of dishes featuring oily fish, such as sardines, mackerel, and clams, which contain the essential omega-3 fatty acids that are considered so important for good health.

The recipes in this book also major on the healthy cooking techniques prevalent in the Spanish cuisine—steaming, braising, grilling, baking, and pan-frying in a minimum of oil. Less healthy techniques traditionally used in some classic recipes have been replaced with a healthier yet equally tasty option. For example, salt cod cakes, which are usually fried, are instead brushed with oil and baked *(see page 32)*.

Fresh ingredients

From the mountains, plains, and seas of Spain comes a wealth of fresh ingredients—luscious fruit and vegetables, creamy cheeses, fresh fish and seafood, and top-quality meats, cured and fresh. Good meat is valued in Spain, a country where purely vegetarian cooking is virtually unknown. However, vegetables are just as essential and many dishes are light on meat—you will often find that just a little chorizo has been added to a vegetable-based dish, for example. Fish and seafood also play a huge role, thanks to Spain's two long coastlines—one bordering the Atlantic and the other the Mediterranean. With the fabulous quality of ingredients, little adornment is necessary and fish and seafood are frequently cooked simply—boiled or grilled over an open fire.

VEGETABLES The warm climate is perfect for growing plump tomatoes, peppery chilies, juicy sweet peppers, and shiny fat eggplants—all of which contribute a vibrant, typically Mediterranean flavor to the cuisine. Onions and garlic are also central to Spanish cooking, while leafy cabbages and tender spinach are beloved across the country. Potatoes, of course, are essential for that classic tapas dish, *patatas bravas (see page 48)*, and they are also added to stews and served as an accompaniment. Another favorite root is the turnip, which is particularly popular in Galicia. Wild mushrooms are a cherished ingredient and are picked throughout the year, particularly in Catalonia and the Basque country. Vegetables are cooked in many ways: served in tapas like *tomates rellenos* (Stuffed Tomatoes, *see page 47*) and *pimientos fritos* (Sautéed Green Sweet Peppers, *see page 44*), added to eggs, or cooked with meat or fish, to name but a few.

HERBS These natural flavorings play an important role in the Spanish kitchen. Robust herbs such as rosemary, thyme, oregano, and bay are used in meat and bean stews, while tender, fragrant fennel is popularly used with seafood, and flat leaf parsley is generously added to all manner of savory dishes.

PORK Pork is one of Spain's most popular meats, not least because of its significance in the country's religious past *(see page 6)*. All families would once have owned a pig, to be fattened up before slaughter and then cured and made into sausages. Of all Spain's sausages, chorizo—spiced and colored red with paprika—is the most widely known. It may be fried, boiled, or added to stews, while the cured sausage can be thinly sliced and served on bread as a tapa. Spain produces some of Europe's finest hams, and about one fifth of the country's pigs are bred for this purpose. *Jamón Serrano* or Serrano ham—named after the Sierra mountains—is one of the most famous. The sweet hams are highly prized and cured with less salt than those produced further south. Fresh pork is also widely used: grilled, added to stews, or made into skewers, as in the classic tapas dish marinated with herbs and spices, *pinchos morunos (see page 52)*.

BEEF The Spanish have never been great beef eaters, preferring to reserve their bulls for fighting, but veal is a popular ingredient. Unlike in other parts of Europe, Spanish veal is not intensively reared. It is braised, pan-fried, or ground and made into meatballs such as *albóndigas (see page 22)*.

LAMB This is traditionally eaten in mountain and grazing regions, and is a classic Easter and wedding treat in other parts of Spain. Chops may be grilled and the legs braised or roasted, while other cuts may be stewed in classic dishes such as the lemon and garlic *cochifrito (see page 106)*.

GAME Wild rabbits thrive across Spain. They form the basis of many stews and braised dishes, and different regions have their own specialties. Wild duck can be found on the lakes and salt flats, and duck shooting is a popular sport. The birds are frequently braised, and often paired with fruit such as oranges and pears. There are literally millions of tiny quail that fly across the country and they make wonderful eating—roasted or casseroled and often cooked with fruit such as raisins or grapes *(see page 102)*.

CHICKEN A favorite throughout the country, there are many regional chicken dishes whose flavoring reflects the area in which the birds are reared. Chicken may be roasted, braised, and stewed, and is frequently teamed with red sweet peppers, oranges, chickpeas, or rice, and flavored with paprika. Sherry or red wine may also be used, according to the region.

FISH Tuna are fished off Gibraltar in the *alamadraba*, an ancient tradition in which men fight the huge fish in the sea. The flesh may be grilled, braised, or stewed and is traditionally used in the fish and potato stew, *marmita-kua (see page 140)*. Mackerel are fished locally and cooked simply, or stewed or pickled in vinegar, as in the Moorish dish *caballa en escabeche (see page 130)*. Sardines are enjoyed in all the coastal regions. On the Malaga coast, the *moraga* festival marks the beginning of summer, when sardines are skewered on sticks and cooked over open fires on the beach.

SHRIMP These are fished on both coasts and several different types are used in the Spanish kitchen. Tiny *camarones* and small Mediterranean shrimp are stirred into numerous dishes and cooked in fritters, while larger pink *gambas* are used in tapas classics such as *gambas al ajillo (see page 20)* and *gambas con romesco (see page 36)*. The larger scampi or jumbo shrimp, which have a wonderful flavor, are perfect for adding to salads.

CRAB This is a delicacy in the coastal regions, particularly on the north coast. Crabs are often boiled and served in their shells, or baked and dressed as in the classic Basque dish *txangurro al horno (see page 139)*. *Txangurro* is the Basque name for the giant spider or spiny crabs that are traditionally used in the dish, which can weigh up to 5 lb or more.

SCALLOPS These are the emblem of Santiago de Compostela and famous in Galicia, where you will find glorious sweet, juicy specimens, large and small. They may be cooked in wine or a tomato sauce, fried or topped with bread crumbs or broiled as in the wonderful *vieiras de Vigo (see page 136)*.

MUSSELS Galicia and Tarragona are important areas for mussels, where they grow on ropes. Many are canned, but fresh ones are also enjoyed—topped with garlic and bread crumbs and grilled as a tapa, steamed open in wine, or added to fish stews such as the classic *zarzuela (see page 142)*.

CLAMS Juicy clams are found in countless dishes, from simple tapas with wine, tomatoes, and herbs to hearty pasta and rice dishes such as *arroz con almejas y vegetales (see page 126)*. They are gathered on both coasts and vary in size from small carpet shell clams to the vast Venus clams.

SQUID AND OCTOPUS Squid is often cooked very quickly until just tender: deep-fried in batter, pan-fried, or griddled as in *calamares a la parilla (see page 34)*. It may also be stuffed and simmered slowly in dishes such as *calamares rellenos (see page 134)*. Octopus suits long, slow simmering and is wonderful in simple dishes such as Galician-style *pulpo a la Gallega (see page 31)* or stews.

CHEESES Spain produces several hundred distinctively flavored cheeses, many regional, from cows', goats', and sheeps' milk. Manchego, made from sheeps' milk, is probably the best known. Made in 6½ lb drums and pressed into grass molds, which give the cheese its patterned rind, it may be sold *semicurado* (under 13 weeks), *curado* (up to 6 months), and *viejo* (over 6 months). The flavor becomes more pronounced with age, with the *curado* bearing similarities to Italian Parmesan.

FRUIT A wonderful selection of fruit thrives in the Spanish climate, from sweet plump apricots to fragrant melons to zesty oranges. Tropical fruits such as kiwi fruit and passion fruit are also grown. Simple fresh fruit is a popular dessert, but desserts may also be created by poaching peaches in wine *(see page 146)* or turning oranges into fruity ices *(see page 152)*.

The Spanish larder

The Spanish pantry is a rich source of ingredients for pairing with fresh produce to create an authentic Spanish flavor—whether for a special paella *(see page 114)*, the classic meat and chickpea stew, *cocido (see page 105)*, or a simple dish of mushrooms sautéed with garlic and olive oil *(see page 96)*.

OLIVES AND OLIVE OIL Cultivated in Spain for millennia, the fruit of the olive tree is one of the joys of Spanish cooking. The fruit is either cured in brine for eating (they are inedible raw) or pressed to extract their rich greenish-gold oil. Olives are marinated and served as a tapa *(see page 41)*, while the oil—with its healthy unsaturated fats—is used for frying, drizzling, and dressings, and imparts a distinctive flavor to dishes.

SPICES The spices used in Spanish cooking have strong roots in the Moorish tradition. Golden saffron was introduced by the Moors and is widely used—in paella, chicken and seafood dishes, as well as in sweet cakes and desserts. The spice is grown in La Mancha and is harvested by hand—hence its high price. Other Moorish spices include coriander and cumin. *Pimentón* or paprika is an everyday spice, used in a similar way to black pepper, and may be mild *(dulce)*, mildly spiced with chili *(picante)*, or bittersweet *(agridulce)*. Cinnamon and nutmeg are other popular spices, particularly for sweet dishes.

RICE Famously grown in Valencia, where it was originally planted by the Moors hundreds of years ago, rice is also grown in Seville and Murcia, and is an important part of the country's cuisine. Spanish rice has short, fat grains and is not dissimilar to Italian risotto rice. It is classically used in paella *(see page 114)*, but this isn't the only rice dish loved by the Spanish. The grain is also used in stuffings, fritters, oven-baked dishes, and soupy stews.

PASTA Made in Andalusia and Catalonia, pasta has been a Spanish staple since the late 18th century. It is used in soups and served with sauces, as in the Catalan dish *fideos a la Catalana (see page 122)*, where the pasta is baked in a rich tomato and sausage sauce.

DRIED BEANS AND LEGUMES These are cooked in hearty, rustic dishes and chickpeas, flageolet and cannellini beans, dried fava beans, and lentils all play an important role in the Spanish kitchen. Frequently cooked with smoky, spicy chorizo, which lends them a particularly delicious flavor, they make popular tapas dishes.

PRESERVED AND CANNED FISH These are an important staple. Probably one of the most distinctive and best-loved preserved fish in Spanish cooking is salt cod, known as *bacalao*. Despite the abundance of fresh fish from the sea, *bacalao* is probably one of the most popular everyday fish eaten in Spain—used in stews, turned into fishcakes *(see page 32)*, served in salads *(see page 64)*, and much more. The hard, board-like pieces of fish must be soaked for at least 24 hours before cooking, both to soften and to remove much of the salt, but once prepared and cooked, it truly is one of the treats of the Spanish table. Canned fish include tuna, which is used in dishes such as the little stuffed pastries, *empanadillas (see page 26)*, served as a tapa, and stuffed eggs, *huevos rellenos (see page 37)*. Anchovies, which are also enjoyed fresh when in season, are a popular Spanish tapa. Usually salted before canning in oil, they may also be brine-pickled or smoked.

Equipment

The basic pots and utensils are all you really need to achieve the routinely fabulous culinary results of the traditional Spanish kitchen. Much traditional cooking is done over an open wood or charcoal fire, but the same effects can be produced with a regular stove. In Spain, the cooking fire would be built on a brick shelf with a metal *plancha* over the top at a working height, with holes for the pots to sit in. Another classic way of cooking is to use a *caldereta*, a fat, round metal pot with three legs that stands over the fire.

Below, the most useful items of Spanish cookware are listed (along with some suggestions for everyday substitutes). These can be bought from specialty cookware stores, mail-order stockists, and over the internet.

PAELLERA This is the classic pan used for cooking paella. Large and flat with two handles and a dimpled base, the *paellera* can range in size from quite small to huge for a large party. Choose a medium one, 10–11 inches in diameter, for cooking for four people. It is important to use the correct size of pan for even distribution of the heat—it should be large enough to hold the rice in a single layer. Otherwise, use a heavy, shallow, flameproof casserole or a heavy skillet or sauté pan of the same size.

PUCHERO This is a large pot for cooking stews that has given its name to many classic Spanish dishes. Depending on the region, the *puchero* may be earthenware and fat and round in shape, or it may be metal with looped handles. These pots are wonderfully durable and heavy-based, to ensure slow, even cooking. Instead, you can use a large, heavy flameproof casserole with a tight-fitting lid—see below—or a good-quality heavy saucepan.

CAZUELAS These classic Spanish earthenware dishes range from tiny individual ones to vast bowls for many people. Glazed on the inside, *cazuelas* are frequently round in shape, but may also be oval. These make perfect oven-to-table cookware and can be used for everything from tapas to large casseroles. To avoid risk of cracking, season a *cazuela* before use by half-filling it with water and a little vinegar and boiling until evaporated. Take the precaution of using a heat diffuser when working with a *cazuela* on the burner, again to avoid cracking.

FLAMEPROOF CASSEROLE This really is a key item of equipment for stewing and braising. A casserole needs to have a heavy base, as well as a heavy, tight-fitting lid to prevent evaporation. These items come in stainless steel or heavy-duty earthenware.

NONSTICK SKILLET This is handy for limiting the amount of oil used when pan-frying. Choose a good-quality pan, which will last much longer than cheap varieties.

HEAVY GRIDDLE PAN This is ideal for cooking meat and fish, and even shellfish, without the need for additional cooking oil, and achieves a delicious chargrilled flavor and appearance. The ridged cast-iron variety is a good choice.

KITCHEN KNIVES A good-quality, large cook's knife is indispensable for preparing ingredients. A small paring knife is also useful for small ingredients, as is a small, serrated knife for cutting tomatoes and fruit.

MORTAR AND PESTLE To make aioli (garlic paste) and tomato paste in the traditional Spanish style, you can use a mortar and pestle instead of a food processor. This piece of equipment is also handy for processing small quantities of other foods.

Preparing seafood
Since Spanish fish and seafood dishes feature fresh ingredients, you will need to know how to prepare them for cooking, although with some items, such as octopus, squid, and scallops, you can ask your fish supplier to do the task for you.

MUSSELS AND CLAMS Scrub the mussels or clams thoroughly, discarding any with damaged shells or those that do not shut when firmly tapped. Pull out any beards attached to the mussels. Put them in a large bowl of cold water and allow to soak for 30 minutes, or 1 hour if large— as in the case of razor clams *(see page 127)*. Drain and use as directed.

OCTOPUS Cut between the head and tentacles of the octopus, just below the eyes. Push the "beak" of the octopus out of the head through the center of the tentacles and discard. Cut the eyes from the head and discard. Clean the head section by slicing through one side, being careful not to damage the ink sac, and scrape out all the guts. Rinse thoroughly under cold running water, pat dry with paper towels and use as directed in the recipe.

SHRIMP To peel, pull off the head and legs, then peel away the shell on the body and tail. To devein, make a shallow cut down the center back, then lift out the black intestinal tract with the tip of the knife and discard.

SARDINES These fish should be scaled and gutted before cooking. Gutting is easy to do: simply cut the head almost through the backbone and then twist, pulling the head toward you. The guts will come away with the head.

SCALLOPS To remove scallops from their shells, grip them firmly with one hand covered with a dish towel, insert a strong, short knife between the two shells and twist firmly to prize the shells apart. Remove and discard the flat, grayish fringe around the scallop, reserving the white flesh and orange coral. If visible, remove and discard the black intestinal tract from the side of the flesh.

SQUID Pull the head and tentacles from the body—the intestines will come away with the head. Remove the squid's wings (the flat pieces of flesh either side of the body), then remove and discard the speckled skin from the body. Remove the skin from the wings, too, if you are using them in the dish. Cut the tentacles from the head, leaving them in one piece, and discard the head and intestines (apart from the ink sac if you want to use the ink). Cut or push out and discard the beak. Remove and discard the transparent bone from the body. Rinse the body, wings, and tentacles under cold running water, pat dry with paper towels and use as directed.

Menu plans

Tapas are traditionally served as a separate event, but they are ideally suited to contemporary lifestyles and our informal approach to dining. Serve them as light brunches or appetizers and starters, as well as nibbles at a drinks party or for a large buffet-style gathering. In more traditional mode, there are one-pot meals that make wonderfully satisfying yet convenient lunches or suppers, perhaps with the addition of a little bread or soup as an appetizer, and there are plenty of main course meat, seafood, or vegetable options to pair with vibrant side dishes or salads. All of these options can be rounded off with a make-ahead dessert.

FAMILY LUNCH 1 FOR 4 PEOPLE

Spinach, Tomato, and Pine Nut Flatbread *(see page 98)*

Eggplant and Mixed Vegetable Stew *(see page 95)*

FAMILY LUNCH 2 FOR 4 PEOPLE

Chicken Soup with Lemon and Mint *(see page 59)*

Baked Eggs with Chorizo, Ham, and Asparagus *(see page 118)*

FAMILY DINNER 1 FOR 4 PEOPLE

Chickpeas with Chorizo *(see page 38)*

Traditional Fish and Potato Stew *(see page 140)*

Spanish-style Green Beans *(see page 81)*

Blood Orange Popsicles *(see page 152)*

FAMILY DINNER 2 FOR 4 PEOPLE

Andalusian-style Salad *(see page 70)*

Catalan-style Noodles with Pork Sausages *(see page 122)*

Catalan-style Spinach *(see page 86)*

Cinnamon Ice Cream *(see page 150)*

SUNDAY LUNCH FOR 4–6 PEOPLE

Andalusian Gazpacho *(see page 62)*

Stuffed Roasted Chicken *(see page 108)*

Spring Vegetable Stew *(see page 82)*

Peaches in Wine *(see page 146)*

SUMMER ALFRESCO MEAL FOR 6–8 PEOPLE

Shrimp in Garlic *(page 20)*

Baked Salt Cod Cakes *(page 32)*

Wrinkled Potatoes *(page 40)*

Andalusian-style Salad *(page 70)*

Peach and Lettuce Salad *(page 68)*

Chilled White Almond and Grape Soup *(page 56)*

Fava Beans with Ham *(page 84)*

Almond and Lemon Cake *(page 149)*

LARGE INFORMAL GATHERING FOR 8–10 PEOPLE

Stuffed Tomatoes *(see page 47)*

Tuna Turnovers *(see page 26)*

Garlic Mushrooms *(see page 30)*

Potatoes with Tomatoes *(see page 48)*

Anchovies with Broiled Red Peppers *(see page 42)*

Piquant Broiled Pork Skewers *(see page 52)*

Rice and Olive Salad *(see page 66)*

Almond and Lemon Cake *(see page 149)*

Stuffed Figs *(see page 148)*

Sparkling Peach Sangria *(see page 156)*

DINNER PARTY FOR 4 PEOPLE

Chilled White Almond and Grape Soup *(see page 56)*

Spanish Rice with Clams and Vegetables *(see page 126)*

Broiled Red Pepper Salad *(see page 68)*

Spanish Custard Creams *(see page 154)*

Stocks

Homemade Spanish stocks do not vary greatly from the stocks used in other Mediterranean cuisines. A good stock needs good ingredients. Vegetables should be scrubbed of all clinging grit and fish bones should be thoroughly rinsed to remove any traces of blood. Chicken carcasses should be trimmed of excess fat. The length of cooking time for various stocks is of prime importance. An overcooked vegetable stock will be bland and tasteless, while an overcooked fish stock will be bitter. The opposite is true for meat stocks, as the longer cooking time enriches their flavor. These stocks can be made and, once cooled, frozen for later use. Freezing them in ice-cube trays is a great way of being able to use just the amount you need for each dish.

Vegetable stock

INGREDIENTS *2 onions, finely chopped* ‖ *2 leeks, trimmed, cleaned, and finely chopped* ‖ *8 celery sticks, finely chopped* ‖ *1 fennel bulb, trimmed and finely chopped* ‖ *2 large carrots, finely chopped* ‖ *2 bay leaves* ‖ *2 thyme sprigs* ‖ *2 flat leaf parsley sprigs* ‖ *1 rosemary sprig* ‖ *½ head of garlic, cut horizontally* ‖ *1 teaspoon black peppercorns* ‖ *3 quarts cold water*

ONE Put all the ingredients in a heavy saucepan and cover them with the measurement water. Bring to a boil, then reduce the heat and simmer gently, uncovered, for 45 minutes. **TWO** Allow to cool slightly before straining through a fine strainer. Allow to cool completely, then store in an airtight container in the refrigerator for up to 1 week or freeze for up to 1 month.

Makes about 8 cups

Chicken stock

INGREDIENTS *2 chicken carcasses, about 4 lb in total* ‖ *6 cups cold water* ‖ *1 onion, quartered* ‖ *1 turnip, roughly chopped* ‖ *1 large carrot, cut into thirds* ‖ *a small bundle of fresh herbs, such as bay leaf, rosemary, thyme, and flat leaf parsley* ‖ *1 teaspoon black peppercorns*

ONE Put the chicken carcasses in a heavy saucepan, cover with the measurement water, and bring to a boil. Add the vegetables, herbs, and peppercorns, then reduce the heat, cover, and simmer gently for 2½ hours. **TWO** Allow to cool slightly before straining through a fine strainer. Allow to cool completely, then store in an airtight container in the refrigerator for up to 2 days or freeze for up to 1 month. Before using the stock, remove and discard any surface fat.

Makes about 4 cups

Fish stock

INGREDIENTS *1 onion, finely chopped* ‖ *1 leek, trimmed, cleaned, and finely chopped* ‖ *4 celery sticks, finely chopped* ‖ *2 lb very fresh fish bones, rinsed and cut into large pieces* ‖ *2 bay leaves* ‖ *2 dill sprigs* ‖ *a few chervil sprigs* ‖ *1 teaspoon white peppercorns* ‖ *1½ cups dry white wine* ‖ *6 cups cold water* ‖ *ice cubes*

ONE Put half the vegetables in a wide, heavy saucepan and spread the fish bones over the top. Cover with the remaining vegetables, herbs, and peppercorns. Add the wine and cover with the measurement water. Bring to a boil, then reduce the heat and simmer gently, uncovered, for 30 minutes, skimming off any scum that rises to the surface frequently and thoroughly. **TWO** Strain through a fine strainer and cool quickly over a bowl of ice. Store in an airtight container in the refrigerator for up to 1 week or freeze for up to 1 month.

Makes about 4 cups

Tapas

Shrimp in garlic *gambas al ajillo*

This is the all-time favorite of tapas bars all over Spain. Fresh crab is sometimes used instead of shrimp in the coastal towns and villages. Serve with crusty bread for mopping up the juices.

INGREDIENTS *8 oz small raw shrimp* ‖ *3 tablespoons olive oil* ‖ *2 garlic cloves, thinly sliced* ‖ *2–3 small dried red chilies, crumbled* ‖ *salt*

ONE Peel the shrimp, leaving the tails intact, then devein *(see page 14)*. Pat them dry with paper towels. **TWO** Heat the oil in a medium *cazuela (see page 13)* over a heat diffuser or heat a shallow, flameproof casserole, add the garlic, chilies, and shrimp and cook over a medium-high heat, stirring, for 2–3 minutes until the shrimp turn pink and are just cooked through. **THREE** Remove from the heat and serve the shrimp immediately in the dish or casserole.

Serves 4

NUTRIENT ANALYSIS PER SERVING 442 kJ – 107 cal – 6 g protein – 1 g carbohydrate – 0 g sugars – 9 g fat – 1 g saturated fat – 0 g fiber – 60 mg sodium

HEALTHY TIP Shrimp are low in fat, while olive oil is rich in beneficial monounsaturated fats. Garlic helps to build up the immune system and prevent the formation of blood clots.

Savory meatballs

albóndigas Moorish in origin, these fragrantly spiced little meatballs are tossed in a paprika-flavored tomato sauce to make another well-loved tapas bar standard. For a variation, replace half the quantity of pork with ground veal.

INGREDIENTS *10 oz ground pork* ‖ *3 garlic cloves, crushed* ‖ *½ cup dried white bread crumbs* ‖ *1 teaspoon ground cumin* ‖ *1 teaspoon ground coriander* ‖ *1 teaspoon ground nutmeg* ‖ *1 teaspoon ground cinnamon* ‖ *2 tablespoons olive oil* ‖ *salt and freshly ground black pepper*

SAUCE *1 tablespoon olive oil* ‖ *1 small onion, finely chopped* ‖ *1 garlic clove, crushed* ‖ *13 oz can chopped tomatoes* ‖ *1 teaspoon golden superfine sugar* ‖ *1 teaspoon pimentón dulce (mild paprika)* ‖ *⅔ cup fresh or frozen peas*

ONE Put the ground meat, garlic, bread crumbs, spices, and salt and pepper to taste in a bowl and, using your fingers, mix together until the mixture is well combined. Cover and chill in the refrigerator for 1 hour to allow the flavors to develop. **TWO** Meanwhile, to make the sauce, heat the oil in a large skillet, add the onion and garlic and cook over a medium heat, stirring frequently, for 5–6 minutes. Stir in the tomatoes and their juice, sugar, and *pimentón* and bring to a boil. Reduce the heat, cover, and simmer gently, stirring occasionally, for 25–30 minutes. Add the peas, season to taste with salt and pepper and cook for 2–3 minutes. **THREE** Take walnut-sized pieces of the ground meat mixture and shape into balls. Heat half the oil in a nonstick skillet, add half the balls and cook over a medium heat, stirring, for 2–3 minutes until browned all over. Remove with a slotted spoon and drain on paper towels. Repeat with the remaining oil and meatballs. **FOUR** Add the meatballs to the sauce over a medium heat, stir to coat evenly, then simmer gently for 5–6 minutes. Serve hot.

Makes about 30

NUTRIENT ANALYSIS PER SERVING 1122 kJ – 266 cal – 20 g protein – 15 g carbohydrate – 6 g sugars – 15 g fat – 3 g saturated fat – 3 g fiber – 164 mg sodium

HEALTHY TIP If using frozen peas, try smaller varieties such as petit pois, as they contain more fiber than larger peas. Frozen peas may have more vitamin content than fresh peas, because they are frozen very soon after picking.

Clams with tomatoes

almejas a la marinera Manzanilla sherry is very pale and dry with a fragrant aroma. Here it is used to bring out the full flavor of the sea in this wonderful dish of clams cooked with fresh tomatoes and parsley. Serve with crusty bread for mopping up the juices.

INGREDIENTS ‖ *2 tablespoons olive oil* ‖ *3 garlic cloves, finely chopped* ‖ *2 ripe tomatoes, finely chopped* ‖ *2 lb live clams, prepared (see page 14)* ‖ *½ cup Manzanilla sherry* ‖ *4 tablespoons finely chopped flat leaf parsley* ‖ *salt and freshly ground black pepper*

ONE Heat the oil in a large skillet, add the garlic and tomatoes and cook, stirring, for 3–4 minutes. **TWO** Add the drained clams to the pan with the sherry and parsley. Season to taste with salt and pepper, then cover tightly and cook over a high heat, shaking the pan vigorously several times, for 4–5 minutes or until all the clams have opened (discard any that remain closed). **THREE** Serve the clams immediately in their cooking liquid or allow to cool to room temperature.

Serves 4

NUTRIENT ANALYSIS PER SERVING 660 kJ – 160 cal – 11 g protein – 5 g carbohydrate – 3 g sugars – 7 g fat – 1 g saturated fat – 1 g fiber – 57 mg sodium

HEALTHY TIP Clams have quite a low fat content and a high proportion of this is present as omega-3 fatty acids, which help to protect against heart disease.

Tuna turnovers *empanadillas de bonito* These small tapa turnovers, which are hugely popular in Spain, are usually deep-fried, but here they are baked until golden to reduce the fat content. You can vary the filling ingredients to use any cooked fish or vegetables of your choice.

INGREDIENTS *1 tablespoon olive oil* ‖ *2 tablespoons very finely chopped onion* ‖ *3 oz cooked, flaked fresh tuna or drained and flaked canned tuna in spring water* ‖ *2 tablespoons finely chopped drained canned pimiento* ‖ *2 tablespoons finely chopped tomato* ‖ *1 tablespoon finely chopped flat leaf parsley* ‖ *2 tablespoons finely chopped hard-cooked egg* ‖ *2 tablespoons organic tomato ketchup* ‖ *8 oz ready-made shortcrust pastry, defrosted if frozen* ‖ *all-purpose flour, for dusting* ‖ *beaten egg, to glaze* ‖ *salt and freshly ground black pepper*

ONE To make the filling, heat the oil in a large, nonstick skillet, add the onion and cook over a low heat, stirring occasionally, for 12–15 minutes until soft and golden. Add the tuna, pimiento, tomato, and parsley and cook over a medium heat, stirring frequently, for 5 minutes. **TWO** Remove the pan from the heat, then add the egg and tomato ketchup and mix well. Season to taste with salt and pepper and allow to cool slightly. **THREE** Roll the pastry out thinly on a lightly floured work surface. Using a 3 inch round plain cookie cutter, stamp out 20 rounds, reusing the trimmings. Line 2 large cookie sheets with nonstick parchment paper and arrange 10 pastry rounds on each one. **FOUR** Put a heaping teaspoonful of the filling into the center of each round and then fold over the pastry to form a turnover. Seal the edges with a fork or crimp with your fingers. Brush each turnover with beaten egg and bake in a preheated oven, 375°F, for 12–15 minutes until golden brown and crisp. Serve warm or at room temperature.

Makes 20

NUTRIENT ANALYSIS PER SERVING 318 kJ – 76 cal – 2 g protein – 7 g carbohydrate – 1 g sugars – 4 g fat – 1 g saturated fat – 1 g fiber – 100 mg sodium

HEALTHY TIP If it's difficult to find tuna canned in spring water, use tuna canned in brine and drain and rinse it before use. Alternatively, use tuna canned in oil and use the drained olive oil for cooking the onion and other ingredients.

Broiled angler fish and caper skewers *banderillas en rape y alcaparra* Broiled fish skewers such as these are found in many of the tapas bars in the coastal regions of Spain. Angler fish has been used here, but you could substitute other firm fish such as fresh tuna, swordfish, or halibut if you prefer.

INGREDIENTS *13 oz angler fish fillet, skinned* ‖ *finely grated zest of 1 lemon* ‖ *juice of ½ lemon* ‖ *1 tablespoon olive oil, plus extra for oiling* ‖ *16 large caperberries* ‖ *8 pimiento-stuffed green olives* ‖ *salt and freshly ground black pepper*

ONE Cut the angler fish into 24 evenly sized pieces and put them in a non-reactive bowl. Mix the lemon zest and juice and oil together in a small pitcher or bowl. Pour over the angler fish and season to taste with salt and pepper. Cover with plastic wrap and allow it to marinate at room temperature for 10 minutes. **TWO** Using 8 bamboo skewers, presoaked in cold water for 30 minutes, or 8 metal ones, thread 3 pieces of angler fish, 2 caperberries, and 1 olive alternately onto each skewer. **THREE** Arrange the skewers on a lightly oiled broiler rack and cook under a preheated high broiler for 3–4 minutes on each side or until the fish is just cooked through. Serve immediately.

Serves 4

NUTRIENT ANALYSIS PER SERVING 570 kJ – 133 cal – 16 g protein – 1 g carbohydrate – 0 g sugars – 7 g fat – 1 g saturated fat – 1 g fiber – 975 mg sodium

HEALTHY TIP Canned or bottled capers and olives prepared in brine will have a high salt content. Rinsing them in water before use will help to reduce the level of sodium in the dish.

Garlic mushrooms *champiñones al ajillo* This classic combination of mushrooms cooked with garlic is made even more special by the addition of sherry. As an alternative to serving the mushrooms hot, with rice or bread, the dish can be left to cool to room temperature and served as a marinated salad.

INGREDIENTS *3 tablespoons olive oil* ‖ *8 oz large mushrooms, such as field or Portobello, trimmed and halved or quartered if very large* ‖ *6 garlic cloves, finely chopped* ‖ *4 tablespoons fino sherry* ‖ *2 tablespoons lemon juice* ‖ *1 teaspoon crushed red pepper* ‖ *a small handful of roughly chopped flat leaf parsley* ‖ *salt*

ONE Heat the oil in a large, nonstick skillet over a high heat and add the mushrooms, stirring constantly. Stir in the garlic, sherry, lemon juice, and crushed red pepper and season to taste with salt. Cook, stirring frequently, for 5–6 minutes. **TWO** Remove from the heat and sprinkle with the chopped parsley. Serve immediately.

Serves 4

NUTRIENT ANALYSIS PER SERVING 436 kJ – 105 cal – 2 g protein – 1 g carbohydrate – 1 g sugars – 9 g fat – 1 g saturated fat – 2 g fiber – 13 mg sodium

HEALTHY TIP Mushrooms contain useful amounts of the trace mineral copper, essential for the healthy growth and repair of bones and connective tissue.

Galician-style octopus *pulpo a la Gallega*

If you don't want to do it yourself, ask your fish supplier to prepare the octopus for you to use in this wonderful tapa, which is a firm favorite throughout the length and breadth of Galicia in northwestern Spain.

INGREDIENTS *1 lb baby octopus, prepared (see page 14)* ‖ *12 black peppercorns* ‖ *2 bay leaves* ‖ *olive oil, for drizzling* ‖ *pimentón dulce (mild paprika), for sprinkling* ‖ *salt* ‖ *chunky lemon wedges, to serve*

ONE Bring a large saucepan of water to a boil over a high heat. Add the octopus, peppercorns, and bay leaves and season to taste with salt. Return to a boil, then reduce the heat to low and simmer very gently, uncovered, for 2 hours or until the octopus is very tender, topping up the water if necessary. **TWO** Remove the octopus from the water, drain well and allow to rest for 10–12 minutes. Using a sharp knife, cut the tentacles into ½ inch thick slices and cut the head into small, bite-size pieces. **THREE** Arrange the octopus on a wooden board and serve drizzled with a little oil, sprinkled with *pimentón* and with lemon wedges for squeezing over.

Serves 4

NUTRIENT ANALYSIS PER SERVING 458 kJ – 110 cal – 17 g protein – 0 g carbohydrate – 0 g sugars – 4 g fat – 0 g saturated fat – 0 g fiber – 5 mg sodium

HEALTHY TIP Octopus is very low in fat. It also contains the trace mineral selenium, essential for the formation of thyroid hormones, as well as a useful amount of copper.

Baked salt cod cakes *buñuelos de bacalao* Usually deep-fried, these delectable

morsels of salt cod and potato are baked for a healthier option. Salt cod was first brought to Spain by the Basque fishermen and is a national food. Serve with a fresh tomato sauce or reduced-fat mayonnaise, if you desire.

INGREDIENTS *10 oz salt cod* ‖ *1¼ cups mashed potatoes, about 10 oz* ‖ *4 green onions, very finely chopped* ‖ *2 garlic cloves, crushed* ‖ *½ cup self-rising flour* ‖ *1 egg, lightly beaten* ‖ *4 tablespoons finely chopped flat leaf parsley* ‖ *olive oil, for brushing* ‖ *freshly ground black pepper* ‖ *lemon wedges, to garnish*

ONE Soak the salt cod in a bowl of cold water overnight, changing the water 3–4 times to remove the excess salt. Drain, put in a large saucepan, cover with fresh cold water and bring to a boil. Reduce the heat to very low and simmer very gently, uncovered, for 30–40 minutes or until the fish is tender. **TWO** Drain the fish, remove and discard the skin and bones and flake the flesh into a bowl. Add the mashed potatoes, green onions, garlic, flour, egg, and parsley to the fish and, using your fingers, mix together until well combined. Cover and chill in the refrigerator for 3–4 hours to allow the flavors to develop. **THREE** Line 1–2 baking sheets with nonstick parchment paper. Shape the fish mixture into small, bite-size balls or cakes and arrange on the prepared baking sheets. Lightly brush the cakes with oil. **FOUR** Bake in a preheated oven, 350°F, for 15–20 minutes or until lightly browned. Serve hot from the oven, garnished with the lemon wedges.

Makes about 30

NUTRIENT ANALYSIS PER SERVING 1130 kJ – 267 cal – 29 g protein – 22 g carbohydrate – 1 g sugars – 8 g fat – 3 g saturated fat – 2 g fiber – 398 mg sodium

HEALTHY TIP Thorough rinsing and draining will considerably reduce the amount of salt in the dish. Cod is low in fat, and fresh tomato sauce will have a lower fat content than even reduced-fat mayonnaise.

Griddled squid

calamares a la parilla *A la parilla* means the method of cooking food on the grill or griddle. In this recipe, succulent baby squid are given this quick and simple yet flavorful treatment.

INGREDIENTS *1 lb prepared baby squid (see page 14)* ‖ *2 tablespoons olive oil, plus extra for oiling* ‖ *finely grated zest and juice of 1 lemon* ‖ *2 garlic cloves, crushed* ‖ *2 tablespoons finely chopped flat leaf parsley* ‖ *salt and freshly ground black pepper*

ONE Put the squid, including the tentacles, in a shallow, non-reactive bowl. Mix the oil, lemon zest and juice, garlic, and parsley together in a small pitcher or bowl. Pour over the squid and season to taste with salt and pepper. Cover with plastic wrap and allow the squid to marinate in the refrigerator for 30 minutes. **TWO** Preheat a broiler until very hot or heat a heavy-based griddle pan over a high heat until smoking. Arrange the squid on a lightly oiled broiler rack and cook under the broiler, turning once, for 2–3 minutes or until just cooked and tender. Alternatively, cook the squid, in batches, in the griddle pan for 2–3 minutes. Remove from the pan and keep hot while cooking the remaining squid. Serve hot.

Serves 4

NUTRIENT ANALYSIS PER SERVING 700 kJ – 169 cal – 19 g protein – 1 g carbohydrate – 0 g sugars – 9 g fat – 1 g saturated fat – 0 g fiber – 220 mg sodium

HEALTHY TIP Squid has a low fat content, most of which is monounsaturated. This sort of fat increases the ratio of "good" HDL cholesterol to "bad" LDL cholesterol in the blood.

Broiled shrimp with romesco sauce

gambas con romesco Romesco is the classic sauce from Catalonia and is made from the famed romesco or nyora red sweet pepper. In this case served with broiled shrimp, the sauce also makes a great dip for vegetable crudités.

INGREDIENTS *20 large raw jumbo shrimp, peeled and deveined (see page 14), with tails left intact*

SAUCE *4 tablespoons olive oil, plus extra for brushing* ‖ *2 oz good-quality white bread, crusts removed* ‖ *1 large red sweet pepper, cored, seeded, and chopped* ‖ *1 dried red chili* ‖ *8 oz ripe tomatoes, chopped* ‖ *4 garlic cloves, crushed* ‖ *3 tablespoons ground almonds* ‖ *3 tablespoons red wine vinegar* ‖ *salt and freshly ground black pepper*

ONE To make the sauce, heat the oil in a large skillet over a medium-high heat. Break the bread into small pieces, add to the pan and fry, stirring, for 2–3 minutes until golden. Remove from the pan with a slotted spoon and drain on paper towels. **TWO** Add the sweet pepper, chili, tomatoes, and garlic to the pan and cook over a medium heat, stirring frequently, for 5–6 minutes. Remove and allow to cool. **THREE** Transfer the fried bread, red pepper mixture, ground almonds, and vinegar to a blender or food processor. Season with salt and pepper, then blend until smooth, adding a little water if the mixture is too thick. Transfer to a bowl, cover, and stand at room temperature for 2–3 hours to let the flavors develop. **FOUR** Arrange the shrimp on a broiler rack and lightly brush with oil. Cook under a preheated high broiler for 2–3 minutes on each side or until they turn pink and are just cooked through. Serve immediately with the sauce for dipping.

Serves 4

NUTRIENT ANALYSIS PER SERVING 934 kJ – 224 cal – 11 g protein – 11 g carbohydrate – 5 g sugars – 15 g fat – 2 g saturated fat – 3 g fiber – 150 mg sodium

HEALTHY TIP Romesco sauce is an excellent source of vitamin C and carotene, both good antioxidants that may help prevent some forms of cancer and are essential to general wellbeing.

Spanish-style tuna-stuffed eggs *huevos rellenos* Stuffed eggs are

popular the world over and are loved by children and adults alike. These are quick and easy to prepare using canned tuna. You can make them with canned salmon if you prefer.

INGREDIENTS *4 hard-cooked eggs* ‖ *3½ oz can tuna in spring water, drained* ‖ *2 tablespoons reduced-fat mayonnaise* ‖ *1 tablespoon tomato paste* ‖ *pinch of pimentón dulce (mild paprika)* ‖ *salt*

TO GARNISH *finely chopped black olives* ‖ *chopped, drained canned pimiento* ‖ *finely chopped flat leaf parsley*

ONE Shell the eggs, then halve lengthwise. Using a teaspoon, carefully scoop out the yolks into a bowl. Put the egg white halves, cut-side up, on a serving plate and set aside. **TWO** Flake the tuna and add to the yolks with the mayonnaise, tomato paste and *pimentón*. Season to taste with salt and pepper and mix together until well combined. **THREE** Using a teaspoon, carefully spoon an equal quantity of the fish mixture into each egg white half. Lightly cover and chill in the refrigerator until ready to serve. **FOUR** Before serving, garnish with chopped black olives, pimiento, and parsley.

Serves 4

NUTRIENT ANALYSIS PER SERVING 590 kJ – 140 cal – 13 g protein – 2 g carbohydrate – 1 g sugars – 9 g fat – 2 g saturated fat – 0 g fiber – 228 mg sodium

HEALTHY TIP Eggs are a nourishing food, rich in protein, iron, and vitamins A and D. They should not be eaten to excess, however, as the egg yolks are high in cholesterol.

Chickpeas with chorizo

garbanzos y chorizo Chickpeas are the most valued legume in Spain. Unlike in the Middle East or India, where chickpeas are used in many forms such as in flour or pastes, the Spanish cook them from dried, after soaking, and then simply stew or boil them and eat them whole. In this hearty tapas dish, canned chickpeas, used for convenience, are cooked with spicy chorizo and ripe tomatoes. Serve with crusty bread.

INGREDIENTS *2 tablespoons olive oil* ‖ *1 red onion, finely chopped* ‖ *2 garlic cloves, crushed* ‖ *7 oz chorizo sausage, cut into ½ inch dice* ‖ *2 ripe tomatoes, seeded and finely chopped* ‖ *3 tablespoons chopped flat leaf parsley* ‖ *2 x 13 oz cans organic chickpeas in water, drained and rinsed* ‖ *salt and freshly ground black pepper*

ONE Heat the oil in a large, nonstick skillet, add the onion, garlic, and chorizo and cook over a medium-high heat, stirring frequently, for 4–5 minutes. **TWO** Add the tomatoes, parsley, and chickpeas to the pan and cook, stirring frequently, for 4–5 minutes until heated through. Season to taste with salt and pepper and serve immediately or allow to cool to room temperature.

Serves 4

NUTRIENT ANALYSIS PER SERVING 1737 kJ – 415 cal – 24 g protein – 36 g carbohydrate – 7 g sugars – 21 g fat – 6 g saturated fat – 10 g fiber – 300 mg sodium

HEALTHY TIP Chickpeas are a great source of dietary fiber and they also contain iron, which is essential for healthy blood. The vitamin C from the tomatoes in this dish will help in the absorption of the iron.

Wrinkled potatoes *papas arrugadas*

This tapa of potatoes simply cooked with a little salt is a Canary Island favorite. It is customarily served with two flavorful sauces or *mojos* for dipping, one green and one red, for which the island is famous.

INGREDIENTS *3 lb baby new potatoes in their skins* ‖ *1 tablespoon sea salt*

GREEN SAUCE *4 tablespoons chopped flat leaf parsley* ‖ *1 green chili, seeded and finely chopped* ‖ *3 garlic cloves, crushed* ‖ *1 teaspoon cumin seeds* ‖ *2 tablespoons olive oil* ‖ *2 tablespoons white wine vinegar* ‖ *salt and freshly ground black pepper*

RED SAUCE *2 tablespoons chopped, drained canned pimiento* ‖ *2 large dried red chilies, seeded and chopped* ‖ *1 tablespoon pimentón dulce (mild paprika)* ‖ *1 teaspoon cumin seeds* ‖ *2 tablespoons olive oil* ‖ *2 tablespoons red wine vinegar* ‖ *salt and freshly ground black pepper*

ONE To make the green sauce, put all the ingredients in a small blender and process until smooth, adding a little water to make a dipping consistency. Season the mixture to taste with salt and pepper and transfer to a serving bowl. Repeat with the ingredients for the red sauce. Alternatively, pound the two different lots of sauce ingredients separately in a mortar with a pestle. **TWO** Transfer each sauce to a separate serving dish, cover, and allow to stand at room temperature for 2–3 hours to let the flavors develop. **THREE** Put the potatoes in a heavy saucepan to fit snugly in a single layer. Pour in enough water to come halfway up the potatoes. Add the sea salt, cover tightly and cook over a low heat for 15–20 minutes or until all the water has evaporated and the potatoes are tender. **FOUR** Uncover the pan and cook for an additional 4–5 minutes until the potato skins start to wrinkle a little. **FIVE** Serve the potatoes warm or at room temperature with the sauces for dipping.

Serves 4

NUTRIENT ANALYSIS PER SERVING 1307 kJ – 309 cal – 6 g protein – 59 g carbohydrate – 4 g sugars – 7 g fat – 1 g saturated fat – 6 g fiber – 1516 mg sodium

HEALTHY TIP Potatoes are a good source of vitamin C, particularly when they are young and have not been stored for very long. Not peeling or scraping the potatoes preserves the vitamin C, as this is found just under the skin.

Spice- and herb-marinated olives

olivos Little bowls of olives grace the counter of every tapas bar in Spain. The olives will be black, green, or purple, and will usually have been cured or marinated, some with spices or garlic and others with chilies. This is a really quick and easy recipe for adding lots of flavor interest to Spanish olives. They can be stored in the refrigerator for up to 2 days.

INGREDIENTS *2 tablespoons red wine vinegar ‖ 3 garlic cloves, thinly sliced ‖ 1 tablespoon coriander seeds ‖ 2 teaspoons cumin seeds ‖ 4 tablespoons finely chopped flat leaf parsley ‖ 1 tablespoon crushed red pepper ‖ 1 teaspoon sweet pimiento ‖ 1 lb mixed green and black olives ‖ olive oil, for drizzling*

ONE Put the vinegar in a small, non-reactive bowl with the garlic, cover with plastic wrap and allow the mixture to soak at room temperature for 24 hours. **TWO** Heat a heavy skillet, add the coriander seeds and dry-fry over a medium heat, stirring, until aromatic and lightly browned. Allow to cool, then coarsely crush in a mortar with a pestle. Toast the cumin seeds in the same way, but leave them whole. **THREE** Drain the garlic, discarding the vinegar, and mix in a separate bowl with the parsley, crushed pepper, sweet pimiento, crushed coriander seeds, and cumin seeds. **FOUR** Add the olives, drizzle over a little oil and toss to mix well. Cover with plastic wrap and allow to marinate at room temperature for 4–5 hours, tossing from time to time, before serving.

Serves 4

NUTRIENT ANALYSIS PER SERVING 540 kJ – 130 cal – 2 g protein – 2 g carbohydrate – 0 g sugars – 14 g fat – 2 g saturated fat – 4 g fiber – 2270 mg sodium

HEALTHY TIP Olives are a great source of monounsaturated fats and the antioxidant vitamin E. They are usually preserved by long soaking in brine, which gives them a high sodium content. You can reduce this to some extent by draining the olives and rinsing them thoroughly before marinating.

Anchovies with broiled red peppers *pimientos del piquillo con anchoas*

Canned red piquillo peppers normally feature in this much-loved tapas dish, but this recipe uses roasted and skinned fresh red bell peppers, combined with the anchovies, to make a delicious snack. Serve with a glass of chilled fino sherry.

INGREDIENTS *3 red bell peppers* ‖ *3½ oz bottle anchovy fillets in salt* ‖ *2 garlic cloves, finely chopped* ‖ *2 tablespoons finely chopped flat leaf parsley* ‖ *extra virgin olive oil, to drizzle*

ONE Arrange the peppers on a broiler rack and cook under a preheated high broiler, turning frequently, for 15–20 minutes or until charred all over. Transfer to a plastic bag and allow to stand for 10–12 minutes for the steam to loosen the skins. **TWO** Carefully peel away the skins, then core and seed the peppers. Cut the flesh into large bite-size pieces and arrange in a single layer in a shallow serving dish. **THREE** Rinse and dry the anchovy fillets, cut them in half lengthwise and arrange them over the peppers in the dish. Sprinkle with the garlic and parsley, and drizzle a little olive oil over the anchovies before serving.

Serves 4

NUTRIENT ANALYSIS PER SERVING 490 kJ –118 cal – 8 g protein – 7 g carbohydrate – 6 g sugars – 7 g fat – 0 g saturated fat – 2 g fiber – 987 mg sodium

HEALTHY TIP Anchovies contain the valuable omega-3 fatty acids thought to be important in the maintenance of levels of "good" HDL cholesterol. Draining and rinsing the anchovies will remove some of the salt content, but not all, so do not add any extra salt to the dish.

Sautéed green sweet peppers *pimientos fritos* From the northwesterly provinces of Spain, these small, green sweet peppers come into the market in spring and summer. They make a delicious appetizer and are best eaten with your fingers. But beware—like Russian roulette, one in every ten of these peppers turns out to be fiery hot! Padrón peppers are available from Spanish markets and suppliers.

INGREDIENTS *13 oz small green sweet Padrón peppers* ‖ *olive oil, for pan-frying* ‖ *sea salt*

ONE Rinse the peppers, leaving the stems intact, and pat dry with paper towels. **TWO** Drizzle a little oil into a large, nonstick skillet and heat over a high heat. Add the peppers to the pan and cook over a medium heat, turning frequently, until lightly browned all over. **THREE** Remove the peppers with a slotted spoon and drain on crumpled paper towels. Transfer to a serving dish and sprinkle with a little sea salt. Serve immediately.

Serves 4–6

NUTRIENT ANALYSIS PER SERVING 268 kJ – 64 cal – 1 g protein – 3 g carbohydrate – 2 g sugars – 6 g fat – 1 g saturated fat – 2 g fiber – 500 mg sodium

HEALTHY TIP Green sweet peppers are a great source of the antioxidant betacarotene, which is believed to protect against cancer, heart disease, and stroke.

Spinach omelet *tortilla de espinacas* A firm tapas favorite, this tortilla also makes for a great meal-in-a-hurry. You could use whatever cooked leftover vegetables you have at hand instead of the spinach if you prefer.

INGREDIENTS *4 cups baby spinach leaves* ‖ *2 tablespoons olive oil* ‖ *1 small onion, finely chopped* ‖ *8 oz potatoes, peeled, cut into ¾ inch dice, cooked until just tender and cooled* ‖ *6 large eggs* ‖ *salt and freshly ground black pepper*

ONE Cook the spinach in a large saucepan of lightly salted boiling water for 1–2 minutes. Drain the spinach thoroughly, squeezing out any excess liquid, then roughly chop. Set aside. **TWO** Heat the oil in an 8 inch nonstick skillet with a flameproof handle (or cover the handle with foil), add the onion and cook over a low heat, stirring occasionally, for 8–10 minutes until softened. Add the potatoes and cook, stirring, for 2–3 minutes. Add the spinach and stir to mix well. **THREE** Lightly beat the eggs in a bowl and season to taste with salt and pepper. Pour into the pan and cook over a low heat, shaking the pan frequently, for 10–12 minutes until it is set on the bottom. **FOUR** Put the pan under a preheated medium broiler and cook for 2–3 minutes or until the top is set and lightly browned. **FIVE** Remove from the heat and allow to rest for 3–4 minutes before turning out onto a cutting board. Cut into wedges or squares and serve.

Serves 4–6

NUTRIENT ANALYSIS PER SERVING 980 kJ – 235 cal – 13 g protein – 13 g carbohydrate – 2 g sugars – 15 g fat – 3 g saturated fat – 3 g fiber – 190 mg sodium

HEALTHY TIP Spinach is a good source of folic acid, the B-group vitamin essential for cell formation. Folic acid can be destroyed by heating, so cook spinach as quickly as possible to preserve its nutritional value.

Stuffed tomatoes *tomates rellenos* These stuffed tomatoes, flavored with garlic and herbs, make a great tapa to serve with drinks. You can also use them to accompany any grilled meat, poultry, or fish dish.

INGREDIENTS *4 large ripe tomatoes* ‖ *2 tablespoons olive oil* ‖ *2 tablespoons pine nuts* ‖ *3 garlic cloves, finely chopped* ‖ *2 cups fresh white bread crumbs* ‖ *1 tablespoon chopped tarragon leaves* ‖ *1 tablespoon chopped flat leaf parsley* ‖ *salt and freshly ground black pepper*

ONE Cut the tomatoes in half widthwise, then scoop out and discard the seeds. Using a small teaspoon, carefully hollow out the tomato shells, reserving the flesh. Arrange the tomato halves, cut-side up, on a baking sheet. **TWO** Heat the oil in a nonstick skillet, add the pine nuts and cook over a medium heat, stirring constantly, for 2–3 minutes. Add the garlic, bread crumbs, and herbs and cook, stirring constantly, for 3–4 minutes. Add the reserved tomato flesh, season to taste with salt and pepper and cook, continuing to stir, for 2–3 minutes. **THREE** Spoon an equal quantity of the mixture into each tomato shell and bake in a preheated oven, 350°F, for 15–20 minutes until the tomatoes have softened. **FOUR** Remove the tomatoes from the oven and allow to cool to room temperature before serving.

Serves 4

NUTRIENT ANALYSIS PER SERVING 755 kJ – 180 cal – 4 g protein – 18 g carbohydrate – 6 g sugars – 11 g fat – 3 g saturated fat – 3 g fiber – 144 mg sodium

HEALTHY TIP Tomatoes are an excellent source of vitamin C and betacarotene. Both of these act as antioxidants, removing free radicals that may cause cancers.

Potatoes with tomatoes *patatas bravas* This classic tapa is a must when

partaking of a little glass of chilled fino sherry in a tapas bar. The potatoes are usually fried, but here they have been oven-roasted instead to reduce the amount of fat required.

INGREDIENTS *1 lb 10 oz potatoes, peeled, cut into bite-size pieces and cooked until just tender* ‖ *olive oil, for drizzling* ‖ *13 oz can chopped tomatoes* ‖ *1 small red onion, finely chopped* ‖ *2 garlic cloves, finely chopped* ‖ *3 teaspoons pimentón dulce (mild paprika)* ‖ *1 bay leaf* ‖ *1 teaspoon golden superfine sugar* ‖ *salt* ‖ *finely chopped flat leaf parsley, to garnish*

ONE Line a baking sheet with parchment paper. Arrange the potatoes in a single layer on the prepared baking sheet. Drizzle over a little oil and season to taste with salt and pepper. Roast in a preheated oven, 425°F, for 15–20 minutes until lightly browned. **TWO** Meanwhile, put the tomatoes and their juice, onion, and garlic in a saucepan and cook over a medium heat, stirring occasionally, for 10–15 minutes. Add the *pimentón*, bay leaf, and sugar and cook, stirring frequently, for an additional 5–10 minutes. **THREE** Transfer the potatoes to a warmed serving dish and pour over the tomato sauce. Toss to mix well and serve, garnished with chopped parsley.

Serves 4

NUTRIENT ANALYSIS PER SERVING 824 kJ – 195 cal – 6 g protein – 40 g carbohydrate – 6 g sugars – 2 g fat – 0 g saturated fat – 4 g fiber – 54 mg sodium

HEALTHY TIP To preserve the vitamin C content of the potatoes, peel them as thinly as possible just before cooking. Garlic and onions may both have a role in the prevention of blood clots, and thus in protection against coronary heart disease.

Mussels with vinaigrette

mejillones en escabeche About 90 percent of the mussels in Spain are harvested off the Galician "sunshine coast." Here they are served as a tapa with a simple vinaigrette dressing. Serve with crusty bread.

INGREDIENTS *2 lb live mussels, prepared (see page 14)* ‖ *3 garlic cloves, finely chopped* ‖ *¾ cup fino sherry* ‖ *6 tablespoons cold water*

VINAIGRETTE *3 tablespoons olive oil* ‖ *2 tablespoons white wine vinegar* ‖ *1 tablespoon very finely chopped shallot* ‖ *1 tablespoon very finely chopped, drained canned or bottled pimiento* ‖ *1 tablespoon very finely chopped parsley* ‖ *salt and freshly ground black pepper*

ONE Put the drained mussels in a large, shallow skillet. Sprinkle with the garlic, sherry, and measurement water. Cover tightly and cook over a high heat, shaking the pan vigorously several times, for 4–5 minutes or until all the mussels have opened (discard any that remain closed). **TWO** Meanwhile, mix all the vinaigrette ingredients together in a small bowl and season to taste with salt and pepper. **THREE** Remove the empty half mussel shells and discard. Arrange the mussels in their half shells in a single layer in a shallow serving dish or use 4 smaller dishes. Spoon the vinaigrette over the mussels and serve immediately.

Serves 4

NUTRIENT ANALYSIS PER SERVING 846 kJ – 200 cal – 13 g protein – 2 g carbohydrate – 1 g sugars – 10 g fat – 1 g saturated fat – 0 g fiber – 165 mg sodium

HEALTHY TIP Mussels contain vitamin B12 and folic acid, and are also a source of selenium and zinc. The trace mineral zinc is essential for the healing of body tissue.

Piquant broiled pork skewers

pinchos morunos Moorish in origin and marinated with herbs and spices, these kebabs can be made from a variety of ingredients, including chicken livers, sausages, and vegetables. This version features lean pork tenderloin.

INGREDIENTS *1 lb lean pork tenderloin*

MARINADE *1 tablespoon chopped thyme leaves* ‖ *1 tablespoon pimentón dulce (mild paprika)* ‖ *2 teaspoons cumin seeds* ‖ *1 tablespoon olive oil, plus extra for oiling* ‖ *juice of 1 lemon* ‖ *salt and freshly ground black pepper*

ONE Cut the pork into ½ inch chunks and put in a non-reactive bowl with all the marinade ingredients. Season to taste with salt and pepper and toss to mix well. Cover with plastic wrap and allow to marinate overnight in the refrigerator. **TWO** When ready to cook, thread the pork onto small bamboo skewers, presoaked in cold water for 30 minutes (about 7–8 pieces of pork to each skewer). **THREE** Arrange the skewers on a lightly oiled broiler rack and cook under a preheated high broiler for 3–4 minutes on each side or until lightly charred and cooked through. Serve immediately.

Serves 4

NUTRIENT ANALYSIS PER SERVING 970 kJ – 230 cal – 26 g protein – 1 g carbohydrate – 0 g sugars – 14 g fat – 4 g saturated fat – 0 g fiber – 98 mg sodium

HEALTHY TIP Pork used to be considered a high-fat meat, but modern rearing methods are producing much leaner cuts. There is still some fat in the muscle meat, giving pork its natural pale color, but if visible fat is removed the meat is only slightly higher in fat than beef or lean lamb.

Eggs with vegetables *piperrada*

This wonderful combination of slowly cooked tomatoes, sweet peppers, and eggplants was thought to have been brought to Europe by the Basques from Mexico, home of the pepper. In this recipe, lightly beaten eggs are stirred into the vegetable mixture, but you can also serve it topped with fried or poached eggs.

INGREDIENTS *2 tablespoons olive oil* ‖ *1 onion, very finely chopped* ‖ *4 garlic cloves, thinly sliced* ‖ *2 red sweet peppers, cored, seeded, and thinly sliced* ‖ *8 oz eggplant, cut into ½ inch dice* ‖ *13 oz can chopped tomatoes* ‖ *1 teaspoon brown sugar* ‖ *4 small eggs* ‖ *salt and freshly ground black pepper* ‖ *chopped flat leaf parsley, to garnish*

ONE Heat the oil in a heavy skillet, add the onion and cook over a low heat, stirring occasionally for 12–15 minutes or until soft and lightly browned. **TWO** Add the garlic, sweet peppers, and eggplant and cook over a medium heat, stirring frequently, for 3–4 minutes. **THREE** Stir in the tomatoes and their juice and sugar, season to taste with salt and pepper and bring to a boil. Reduce the heat, cover, and cook over a low heat for 25–30 minutes until the mixture has thickened. **FOUR** Lightly beat the eggs and stir them into the pan. Remove the pan from the heat, cover, and allow the eggs to stand for 5–6 minutes or until they are just set. **FIVE** Sprinkle with chopped parsley to garnish and serve immediately in little bowls as a tapa or in the pan as a main course.

Serves 4 as a tapa or 2 as a main course

NUTRIENT ANALYSIS PER SERVING 840 kJ – 200 cal – 10 g protein – 14 g carbohydrate – 13 g sugars – 12 g fat – 3 g saturated fat – 4 g fiber – 122 mg sodium

HEALTHY TIP Eggs are an excellent source of protein and iron for non-meat eaters. The tomatoes and peppers in the recipe are rich in vitamin C, which helps the absorption of iron.

Soups and salads

Chilled white almond and grape soup *ajo blanco con uvas*

This pale chilled soup is the perfect appetizer for a really hot summer's day lunch or dinner. Use the best-quality Spanish almonds you can find for a superior flavor.

INGREDIENTS *4 slices of day-old bread, crusts removed, broken into pieces* ‖ *⅔ cup whole blanched almonds* ‖ *2 garlic cloves, finely chopped* ‖ *4 tablespoons extra virgin olive oil, plus extra for drizzling* ‖ *4 tablespoons red wine vinegar* ‖ *4 cups iced water* ‖ *½ cup peeled seedless white or green grapes, roughly chopped* ‖ *salt*

ONE Soak the bread in a bowl of cold water for 5–6 minutes. **TWO** Meanwhile, put the almonds in a food processor with the garlic and process in bursts until finely ground. **THREE** Drain the bread and squeeze out the excess liquid Add to the almond mixture and process until smooth. Add the oil and vinegar and continue to process until smooth. With the machine running, pour in the measurement iced water in a thin stream and process until smooth. **FOUR** Strain the mixture through a fine sieve, pressing down hard to extract as much liquid as you can. Season to taste with salt, cover, and chill in the refrigerator for 8–10 hours or overnight. **FIVE** Just before serving, pour the mixture into individual chilled bowls and top each bowl with an equal quantity of the grapes. Drizzle with olive oil and serve immediately.

Serves 4

NUTRIENT ANALYSIS PER SERVING 1470 kJ – 353 cal – 8 g protein – 21 g carbohydrate – 6 g sugars – 27g fat – 3 g saturated fat – 2 g fiber – 163 mg sodium

HEALTHY TIP Almonds contain high levels of vitamin E, as well as useful amounts of B vitamins and some minerals. Grapes provide carotene, which the body uses to make vitamin A, as well as small amounts of B vitamins and vitamin C.

Galician-style broth _caldo Gallego_ This hearty vegetable and meat soup from Galicia is cooked all together in one pot. It traditionally uses salt pork, but lean bacon has been substituted here for a healthier version.

INGREDIENTS _2½ quarts cold water_ ‖ _1 cup white navy beans, soaked overnight in cold water and drained_ ‖ _4 oz lean bacon, in one piece_ ‖ _4 oz Serrano ham, in one piece_ ‖ _8 oz stewing beef, in one piece_ ‖ _2 onions, thickly sliced_ ‖ _12 oz potatoes, peeled and quartered_ ‖ _4 small white turnips, peeled and halved_ ‖ _2½ cups chopped green cabbage_ ‖ _salt and freshly ground black pepper_

ONE Put the measurement water in a large, heavy saucepan with the beans, bacon, ham, beef, and onions. Bring to a boil, skimming off any foam that rises to the surface. Reduce the heat, cover, and cook over a very low heat for about 1½ hours. **TWO** Add the potatoes and turnips, re-cover and cook for 20–25 minutes or until tender. Add the cabbage, re-cover and cook for an additional 10 minutes. Season to taste with salt and pepper and remove from the heat. **THREE** Remove the meats with a slotted spoon and cut into bite-size portions. Ladle the soup into large warmed bowls and top with the meats. Serve immediately.

Serves 4

NUTRIENT ANALYSIS PER SERVING 1873 kJ – 444 cal – 40 g protein – 50 g carbohydrate – 11 g sugars – 10 g fat – 3 g saturated fat – 17 g fiber – 1280 mg sodium

HEALTHY TIP The addition of potatoes and navy beans makes this a highly nutritious one-pot meal, with a balanced combination of proteins and carbohydrate. Avoid adding additional salt, as the ham and bacon mean that the sodium level is already quite high.

Chicken soup with lemon and mint *canja* Popular in both

Spain and Portugal, this clear chicken soup, which has been flavored with fresh mint and lemon, is comfort food at its best.

INGREDIENTS *1 small whole chicken, about 2 lb, jointed* ‖ *8 cups water or store-bought or homemade Vegetable Stock (see page 16)* ‖ *2 onions, finely chopped* ‖ *1 bay leaf* ‖ *3 tablespoons paella rice, such as Calasparra or Bomba, or other short-grain rice* ‖ *2 tablespoons lemon juice* ‖ *8 tablespoons finely chopped fresh mint leaves* ‖ *salt and freshly ground black pepper*

ONE Put the chicken in a large, flameproof casserole with the measurement water or stock, onions, and bay leaf and bring it to a boil. Reduce the heat, cover tightly, and cook over a very low heat for 30 minutes. **TWO** Stir in the rice, re-cover and cook for an additional 1 hour. Remove from the heat and allow the chicken to cool in the stock. **THREE** Remove the chicken from the stock with a slotted spoon. Remove and discard the skin and bones. Tear the flesh into bite-size pieces and return to the casserole. Stir in the lemon juice and reheat the soup until hot. Season to taste with salt and pepper. **FOUR** Add the mint and stir well. Ladle into warmed bowls and serve immediately.

Serves 4

NUTRIENT ANALYSIS PER SERVING 1787 kJ – 430 cal – 32 g protein – 17 g carbohydrate – 4 g sugars – 26 g fat – 8 g saturated fat – 1 g fiber – 129 mg sodium

HEALTHY TIP When the chicken and stock have cooled, skim as much fat from the surface as you can. Alternatively, remove the skin from the chicken before starting the cooking process.

15-minute soup *sopa al cuarto de hora* This Iberian soup makes use of both fresh and pantry ingredients for a fantastically quick yet satisfying afterwork supper. It is ideal followed by a crisp green salad.

INGREDIENTS *2 tablespoons olive oil* ‖ *1 small onion, finely chopped* ‖ *2 garlic cloves, finely chopped* ‖ *2 thick slices of day-old bread, crusts removed, broken into pieces* ‖ *2 tomatoes, roughly chopped* ‖ *4 cups store-bought or homemade Vegetable Stock (see page 16)* ‖ *1⅓ cups frozen peas* ‖ *1 teaspoon pimentón dulce (mild paprika)* ‖ *½ cup fino sherry* ‖ *8 oz raw jumbo shrimp in their shells* ‖ *1 hard-cooked egg, shelled and finely chopped* ‖ *2 tablespoons finely chopped flat leaf parsley* ‖ *salt and freshly ground black pepper*

ONE Heat the oil in a medium saucepan, add the onion, garlic, and bread and cook over a medium heat, stirring frequently, for 3–4 minutes. **TWO** Add the tomatoes, stock, peas, *pimentón*, and sherry and bring to a boil. Reduce the heat and cook over a medium heat, stirring occasionally, for 3–4 minutes. **THREE** Add the shrimp and cook, stirring frequently, for 5–7 minutes or until the shrimp turn pink and are just cooked through. Remove from the heat and season to taste with salt and pepper. **FOUR** Ladle into warmed shallow bowls, sprinkle with the egg and parsley and serve immediately.

Serves 4–6

NUTRIENT ANALYSIS PER SERVING 1000 kJ – 239 cal – 15 g protein – 20 g carbohydrate – 5 g sugars – 8 g fat – 2 g saturated fat – 5 g fiber – 240 mg sodium

HEALTHY TIP Consuming onions and garlic may help to prevent blood clotting and heart disease. Onions also contain allicin and sulforaphane, which may reduce the risk of some cancers.

Andalusian gazpacho

gazpacho Andaluz This classic chilled soup, deliciously refreshing on a hot summer's day, was traditionally made in a Spanish mortar or *mortero*. However, in today's world, a blender or food processor takes all the hard work out of the preparation without compromising the flavor of the original.

INGREDIENTS *2 lb vine-ripened tomatoes* ‖ *2 slices of day-old crusty bread* ‖ *1 red sweet pepper, cored, seeded, and roughly chopped* ‖ *2 garlic cloves, finely chopped* ‖ *1 teaspoon golden superfine sugar* ‖ *2–3 tablespoons red wine vinegar* ‖ *2–3 tablespoons extra virgin olive oil* ‖ *a few drops of Tabasco sauce* ‖ *salt and freshly ground black pepper*

OVEN-BAKED CROUTONS *2 thick slices of bread* ‖ *olive oil, for brushing*

GARNISH TOPPINGS *4 tablespoons finely diced cucumber* ‖ *3 tablespoons finely diced red onion* ‖ *chopped flat leaf parsley*

ONE Score a cross in the base of each tomato. Put in a heatproof bowl, pour over boiling water to cover and leave for 10–15 seconds. Drain and plunge into cold water, then peel away the skins. Cut the tomatoes in half. Seed and roughly chop the flesh, then transfer to a blender or food processor. **TWO** Break the bread into pieces and soak in a bowl of cold water for 5–6 minutes, then drain and squeeze out the excess liquid. Add to the tomatoes in the blender or food processor with the sweet pepper, garlic, sugar, vinegar, oil, and Tabasco. Blend until smooth, adding a little chilled water if you want a thinner consistency. Season to taste with salt and pepper, then transfer to a bowl. Cover and chill in the refrigerator for 3–4 hours. **THREE** Meanwhile, to make the croutons, remove the crusts from the bread and cut the bread into cubes. Lightly brush a baking sheet with oil. Spread the bread cubes out on the baking sheet and brush lightly with oil. Bake in a preheated oven, 400°F, for 10–15 minutes until golden and crisp. Transfer to a wire rack and allow to cool. **FOUR** To serve, ladle the gazpacho into chilled bowls and top with a little of each of the garnish toppings and the croutons. Serve the remainder in small bowls for people to help themselves.

Serves 4–6

NUTRIENT ANALYSIS PER SERVING 1070 kJ – 254 cal – 7 g protein – 36 g carbohydrate – 12 g sugars – 10 g fat – 2 g saturated fat – 6 g fiber – 286 mg sodium

HEALTHY TIP Tomatoes and peppers are brilliant sources of vitamin C and betacarotenes, both very important for their antioxidant properties. Tomatoes also contain lycopene, a pigment that produces the tomato's red color and which may help to protect against bladder and pancreatic cancers.

Salad of salt cod with tomatoes and peppers *ensalada de bacalao*

Salt cod is highly esteemed in Spanish cooking and here it is used to make a robust and colorful salad that is substantial enough to serve as a main course.

INGREDIENTS *13 oz salt cod* ‖ *2 red sweet peppers, cored, seeded, and thinly sliced* ‖ *4 ripe tomatoes, thinly sliced* ‖ *juice of 1 lemon* ‖ *extra virgin olive oil, for drizzling* ‖ *freshly ground black pepper* ‖ *chopped flat leaf parsley, to garnish*

ONE Soak the cod in a bowl of cold water overnight, changing the water 3–4 times to remove the excess salt. **TWO** Drain, put in a large saucepan, cover with fresh cold water and bring to a boil. Reduce the heat and simmer over a low heat for 15–20 minutes or until tender. **THREE** Drain the fish, remove and discard the skin and bones and coarsely flake the flesh. Transfer to a shallow salad bowl. **FOUR** Mix the sweet peppers and tomatoes together and add to the fish. Toss to mix well. **FIVE** Pour over the lemon juice and drizzle a little oil over the salad. Season to taste with pepper and sprinkle with chopped parsley before serving.

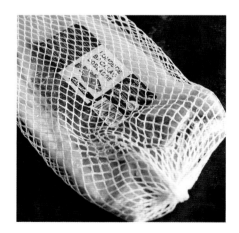

Serves 4

NUTRIENT ANALYSIS PER SERVING 790 kJ – 186 cal – 34 g protein – 7 g carbohydrate – 7 g sugars – 3 g fat – 1 g saturated fat – 2 g fiber – 410 mg sodium

HEALTHY TIP Salt cod is low in fat. It is complemented in this recipe by the addition of peppers and tomatoes, both high in antioxidants. These are thought to prevent cancers by removing the possibly carcinogenic free radicals found naturally in some foods and created through the cooking process in others.

Rice and olive salad *ensalada de arroz* This salad is a great way to use up
leftover cooked rice and makes an ideal colorful, fresh, and tasty addition to any picnic or summer lunch.

INGREDIENTS *3 cups cold cooked long-grain white rice* ‖ *4 green onions, finely chopped* ‖ *1 garlic clove,*
very finely chopped ‖ *1 red sweet pepper, cored, seeded, and very finely chopped* ‖ *15 black olives, pitted*
and finely chopped ‖ *15 green olives, pitted and finely chopped* ‖ *12 cherry tomatoes, halved* ‖
4 tablespoons chopped flat leaf parsley ‖ *juice of 1 lemon* ‖ *2 tablespoons olive oil* ‖ *salt and freshly*
ground black pepper

ONE Put the rice in a shallow salad bowl and fluff up the grains with a fork to separate. **TWO** Add the green
onions, garlic, sweet pepper, olives, tomatoes, and parsley and stir to mix well. **THREE** Pour over the lemon
juice and drizzle over the oil. Season to taste with salt and pepper and toss to mix well. Serve immediately.

Serves 4

NUTRIENT ANALYSIS PER SERVING 1000 kJ – 239 cal – 4 g protein – 35 g carbohydrate – 5 g sugars –
10 g fat – 2 g saturated fat – 4 g fiber – 855 mg sodium

HEALTHY TIP Olives are rich in monounsaturated fat, which can help to maintain a higher ratio of "good"
HDL cholesterol to "bad" LDL cholesterol and so possibly avert cardiovascular disease. To reduce the salt
content of olives preserved in brine, rinse well and drain.

Broiled red pepper salad

ensalada de pimientos morrones This colorful and delicious salad makes a great appetizer or terrific accompaniment to any fish, chicken, or meat dish.

INGREDIENTS *4 red sweet peppers*

DRESSING *1 garlic clove, crushed* ‖ *3 tablespoons red wine vinegar* ‖ *4 tablespoons olive oil* ‖ *salt and freshly ground black pepper*

ONE Arrange the peppers on a broiler rack and cook under a preheated high broiler, turning frequently, for 15–20 minutes or until charred all over. Transfer to a plastic bag and allow to stand for 10–12 minutes for the steam to loosen the skins. **TWO** Carefully peel away the skins, then core and seed the peppers. Arrange in a shallow bowl in a single layer. **THREE** To make the dressing, mix all the ingredients together in a small pitcher or bowl, season to taste with salt and pepper and pour over the peppers. Cover and allow to stand at room temperature for 10–15 minutes to let the flavors develop before serving.

Serves 4

NUTRIENT ANALYSIS PER SERVING 597 kJ – 144 cal – 2 g protein – 9 g carbohydrate – 9 g sugars – 12 g fat – 2 g saturated fat – 3 g fiber – 8 mg sodium

HEALTHY TIP Red sweet peppers are a particularly good source of vitamin C. This vitamin is essential for the maintenance and repair of body tissue, and it is also invaluable for its antioxidant properties.

Peach and lettuce salad

ensalada de melocotones This peach and lettuce salad is a popular Majorcan appetizer in hot weather. Substitute fresh ripe apricots for the peaches if you desire.

INGREDIENTS *1 lb ripe peaches* ‖ *4 Little Gem or small crisp head lettuces* ‖ *¾ cup low-fat plain yogurt* ‖ *6 tablespoons reduced-fat mayonnaise* ‖ *2 tablespoons chopped almonds, toasted* ‖ *salt and freshly ground black pepper*

ONE Bring a large saucepan of water to a boil. Add the peaches and leave for 30 seconds. Drain and plunge into cold water, then peel away the skins. **TWO** Cut each peach in half, remove and discard the pits, and cut each half into 4 wedges. **THREE** Separate the leaves of the lettuces and arrange around the edge of a salad platter, then put the peach slices in the center of the dish. **FOUR** Beat the yogurt and mayonnaise together in a small bowl, season to taste with salt and pepper and spoon over the salad. Sprinkle with the almonds just before serving.

Serves 4

NUTRIENT ANALYSIS PER SERVING 830 kJ – 198 cal – 8 g protein – 16 g carbohydrate – 15 g sugars – 12 g fat – 1 g saturated fat – 5 g fiber – 257 mg sodium

HEALTHY TIP Folic acid is found in varying quantities in most vegetables (particularly leafy green ones) and some fruit. Lettuce, especially the greener outer leaves, is an excellent source. Folic acid is essential for the development and maintenance of body cells.

Andalusian-style salad

ensalada a la Andaluza Typical of this region's approach to hot-weather dining, this wonderfully colorful and refreshing summer salad makes a great start to a summer meal.

INGREDIENTS *4 ripe tomatoes, sliced or quartered* ‖ *1 red onion, halved and very thinly sliced* ‖ *2 red sweet peppers, cored, seeded, and thinly sliced* ‖ *16 green olives, pitted* ‖ *4 tablespoons olive oil* ‖ *3 tablespoons sherry vinegar* ‖ *1 teaspoon honey* ‖ *1 garlic clove, crushed* ‖ *salt and freshly ground black pepper* ‖ *finely chopped flat leaf parsley, to garnish*

ONE Put the tomatoes, onion, sweet peppers, and olives together in a shallow salad bowl or on a salad platter. **TWO** Mix the oil, vinegar, honey, and garlic in a small pitcher or bowl. Season to taste with salt and pepper and pour over the salad. Toss to mix well. **THREE** Cover and allow to stand at room temperature for 15–20 minutes to let the flavors develop, then serve, garnished with chopped parsley.

Serves 4

NUTRIENT ANALYSIS PER SERVING 772 kJ – 186 cal – 2 g protein – 14 g carbohydrate – 13 g sugars – 14 g fat – 2 g saturated fat – 4 g fiber – 440 mg sodium

HEALTHY TIP Red sweet peppers are a very rich source of carotene, which the body converts to vitamin A. They are also very high in vitamin C, making this salad an extremely good source of antioxidants, thought to be important in the prevention of cancers.

Red onion and orange salad
ensalada de cebolla y naranjas This vibrant salad with tangy and sweet notes, fragrant with fresh mint, will bring a splash of sunshine to any table. It should always be served chilled.

INGREDIENTS *4 tablespoons golden raisins* ‖ *4 large sweet oranges* ‖ *1 small red onion, thinly sliced* ‖ *20 black olives, pitted* ‖ *2 tablespoons slivered almonds* ‖ *a small handful of mint leaves* ‖ *2 tablespoons red wine vinegar* ‖ *4 tablespoons olive oil* ‖ *salt and freshly ground black pepper*

ONE Soak the raisins in a bowl of hot water for 20 minutes to plump up. Drain and transfer to a shallow salad bowl or salad platter. **TWO** Remove the skin and pith from the oranges. Working over a bowl to catch the juice, cut between the membranes to remove the segments. **THREE** Add the orange segments to the bowl or platter with the onion, olives, almonds, and mint and toss to mix well. **FOUR** Mix the vinegar and oil together in a small pitcher or bowl with the reserved orange juice and season to taste with salt and pepper. Pour over the salad and toss to coat evenly. Cover and chill in the refrigerator for 1–2 hours before serving.

Serves 4

NUTRIENT ANALYSIS PER SERVING 1375 kJ – 328 cal – 5 g protein – 40 g carbohydrate – 40 g sugars – 17 g fat – 2 g saturated fat – 8 g fiber – 385 mg sodium

HEALTHY TIP This is a very nutritious salad. Oranges have a high vitamin C content and are also a good source of folic acid. Almonds are a good source of vitamin E, and both almonds and raisins contain useful amounts of iron.

Potato and vegetable salad

ensaladilla rusa This salad is served throughout Spain with little variation. It is a perfectly balanced mixture of potatoes, eggs, and vegetables, lightly dressed with mayonnaise to accent the different flavors.

INGREDIENTS *13 oz potatoes, peeled and cut into ¾ inch dice* ‖ *1 large carrot, cut into ¾ inch dice* ‖ *⅔ cup fresh or frozen peas* ‖ *1 cup green beans, trimmed and cut into ¾ inch lengths* ‖ *½ onion, finely chopped* ‖ *1 small red sweet pepper, cored, seeded, and very finely chopped* ‖ *2 tablespoons finely chopped gherkins* ‖ *1 tablespoon small capers* ‖ *12 pimiento-stuffed green olives* ‖ *chopped flat leaf parsley, to garnish*

DRESSING *⅔ cup low-fat mayonnaise* ‖ *1 tablespoon lemon juice* ‖ *1 teaspoon Dijon mustard* ‖ *salt and freshly ground black pepper*

ONE Bring a large saucepan of lightly salted water to a boil, add the potatoes and carrots and cook for 10–12 minutes or until almost tender. Add the peas and beans and cook for 1–2 minutes. **TWO** Drain the vegetables and transfer to a shallow salad bowl with the onion, sweet pepper, gherkins, capers, and olives. **THREE** Beat all the dressing ingredients together in a small bowl and season to taste with salt and pepper. Spoon over the salad and toss to coat evenly (you may need to do this with your fingers). **FOUR** Garnish with chopped parsley before serving.

Serves 4

NUTRIENT ANALYSIS PER SERVING 988 kJ – 236 cal – 5 g protein – 27 g carbohydrate – 9 g sugars – 13 g fat – 0 g saturated fat – 6 g fiber – 796 mg sodium

HEALTHY TIP Most of the vitamin C in potatoes is near the surface of the skin, so peel them as thinly as possible. Vitamin loss will also be reduced if you use a sharp knife.

Apple and walnut salad *ensalada de manzana y nueces* As well as being sweet and delicious, this combination of apple, walnuts, and celery is full of crisp and crunchy texture. Serve with a chilled glass of fino sherry for maximum enjoyment.

INGREDIENTS *1 crisp apple, such as Granny Smith* ‖ *4 green onions, thinly sliced* ‖ *2 tablespoons raisins* ‖ *2 celery sticks, thinly sliced* ‖ *¾ cup chopped walnuts* ‖ *8 oz potato, peeled, cut into ¾ inch dice and cooked until just tender* ‖ *1 tablespoon lemon juice* ‖ *⅔ cup low-fat mayonnaise* ‖ *½ cup low-fat plain yogurt* ‖ *1 tablespoon finely chopped cilantro* ‖ *salt and freshly ground black pepper*

ONE Core and cut the apple into thin slices. Put in a salad bowl with the green onions, raisins, celery, walnuts, and potato. **TWO** Beat the lemon juice, mayonnaise, and yogurt together in a small bowl. Season to taste with salt and pepper, spoon over the salad and toss to coat evenly. Sprinkle with the cilantro and serve immediately.

Serves 4

NUTRIENT ANALYSIS PER SERVING 1644 kJ – 395 cal – 8 g protein – 30 g carbohydrate – 20 g sugars – 28 g fat – 1 g saturated fat – 4 g fiber – 386 mg sodium

HEALTHY TIP Most of the fat in walnuts is polyunsaturated, so these nuts are a useful ingredient for those aiming at a diet low in saturated fats. Walnuts are not as high in vitamin E as some other nuts, but they do also contain small amounts of B vitamins.

Leek salad *ensalada de puerros* This attractive salad comes from the Basque region. Try to use baby leeks that are as fresh as possible to add sweetness to the dish.

INGREDIENTS *20–24 baby leeks, trimmed, halved lengthwise, and cleaned* ‖ *4 tablespoons olive oil* ‖ *2 tablespoons red wine vinegar* ‖ *1 garlic clove, crushed* ‖ *1 teaspoon pimentón dulce (mild paprika)* ‖ *2 hard-cooked eggs, shelled and finely chopped* ‖ *salt and freshly ground black pepper*

ONE Bring a large saucepan of lightly salted water to a boil, add the leeks and cook for 8–10 minutes or until tender. Drain thoroughly and arrange in a shallow salad bowl. **TWO** Mix the oil, vinegar, garlic, and *pimentón* together in a small pitcher or bowl. Season to taste with salt and pepper and pour over the leeks. Sprinkle with the hard-cooked eggs and serve immediately.

Serves 4

NUTRIENT ANALYSIS PER SERVING 740 kJ – 179 cal – 6 g protein – 5 g carbohydrate – 3 g sugars – 15 g fat – 3 g saturated fat – 4 g fiber – 46 mg sodium

HEALTHY TIP Leeks are quite high in carotene (used by the body to make vitamin A) and also contain folic acid, particularly in the dark green parts of the vegetable. Folic acid is heat-sensitive, so try to cook green vegetables for as short a time as possible.

Vegetables

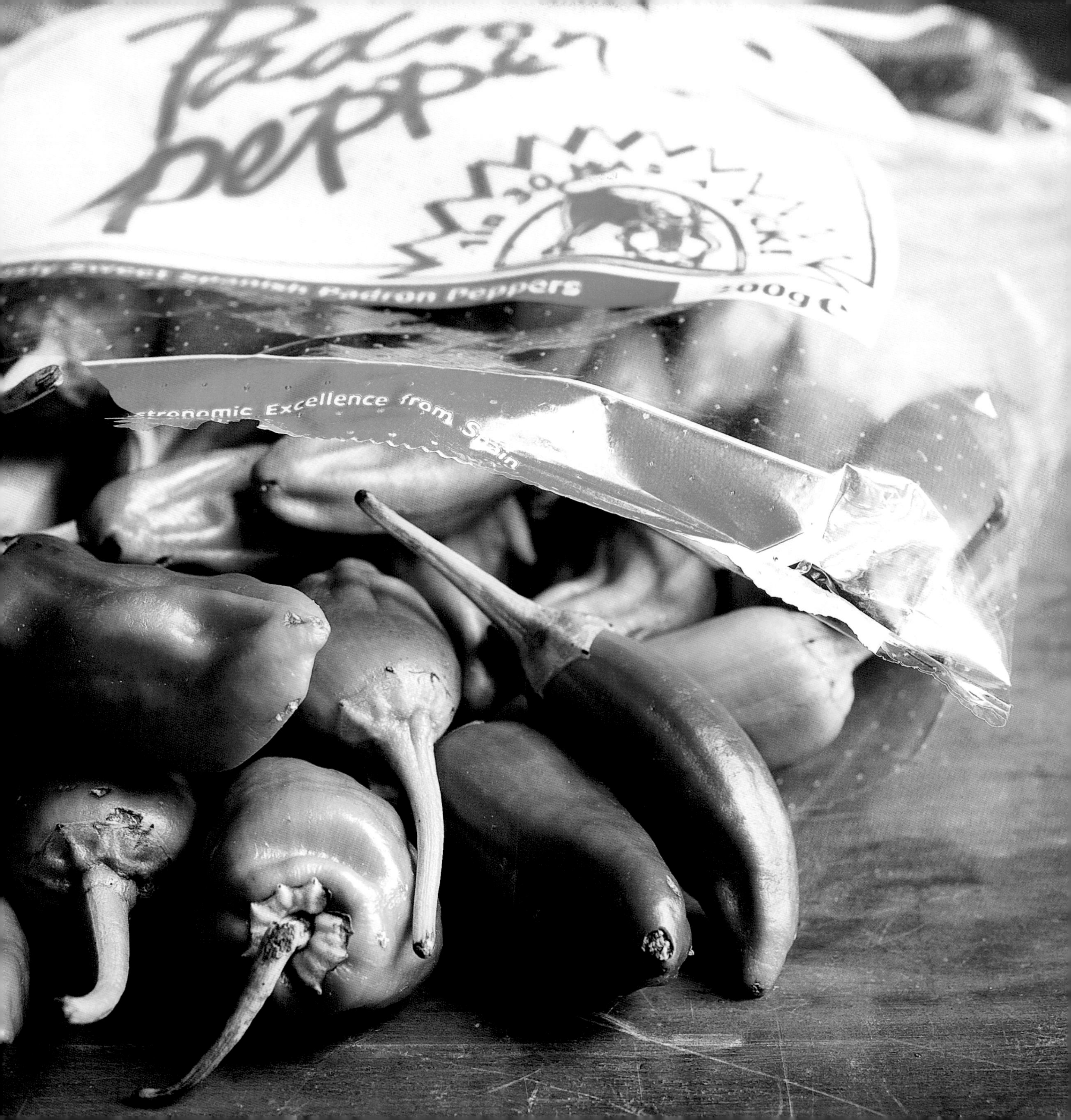
Padron Peppers
200g
Excellence from

Fennel gratin *sopa de hinojo*

Fresh Spanish curd cheese from the Balearic islands is called *queso tierno*. Here it is used to top the fennel for this simple and delicious gratin. You can use any white fresh curd cheese or ricotta instead. Alternatively, try *rollito de cabra*, a soft mature goats' milk cheese from Extremadura.

INGREDIENTS *13 oz baby fennel or 2 fennel bulbs* ‖ *6 tablespoons fresh curd cheese or ricotta* ‖ *1 tablespoon chopped oregano leaves, plus extra whole leaves to garnish* ‖ *olive oil, for drizzling* ‖ *salt and freshly ground black pepper*

ONE Trim and halve the baby fennel or thickly slice the fennel bulbs. Bring a large saucepan of lightly salted water to a boil, add the fennel and cook for 15–20 minutes. Drain and arrange in a shallow gratin dish in a single layer. **TWO** Spoon over the cheese and sprinkle with the oregano. Season to taste with salt and pepper and drizzle with a little oil. Cook under a preheated medium-high broiler for 6–8 minutes or until lightly golden. Serve immediately, garnished with whole oregano leaves.

Serves 4

NUTRIENT ANALYSIS PER SERVING 259 kJ – 62 cal – 3 g protein – 2 g carbohydrate – 2 g sugars – 5 g fat – 2 g saturated fat – 2 g fiber – 36 mg sodium

HEALTHY TIP Although folic acid is usually found in leafy dark green vegetables, fennel—a pale-colored bulb—contains significant amounts of this B-group vitamin. Folic acid helps ward off anemia and it is vital for cell formation, especially during the earliest stages of life.

Garlicky cauliflower

coliflor al ajillo Typical of dishes from the Navarre and Rioja regions of Spain, this simple yet aromatic treatment transforms the humble cauliflower into something fresh and exciting. This recipe would work equally well with broccoli.

INGREDIENTS *2½ cups cauliflower florets* ‖ *4 tablespoons olive oil* ‖ *3 garlic cloves, finely chopped* ‖ *1 tablespoon pimentón dulce (mild paprika)* ‖ *2 tablespoons white wine vinegar* ‖ *salt and freshly ground black pepper* ‖ *finely chopped flat leaf parsley, to garnish*

ONE Bring a large saucepan of lightly salted water to a boil. Break the cauliflower florets into bite-size pieces, add to the pan and cook for 6–8 minutes. Drain thoroughly and set aside. **TWO** Heat the oil in a large, nonstick skillet. Add the garlic and cook over a medium heat, stirring, for 1–2 minutes. Add the cauliflower, *pimentón*, and vinegar and season to taste with salt and pepper. Cook over a high heat, stirring, for 3–4 minutes, then remove from the heat. Sprinkle with some chopped flat leaf parsley to garnish and serve immediately.

Serves 4

NUTRIENT ANALYSIS PER SERVING 716 kJ – 173 cal – 8 g protein – 7 g carbohydrate – 5 g sugars – 13 g fat – 2 g saturated fat – 4 g fiber – 20 mg sodium

HEALTHY TIP Cauliflower provides folic acid and vitamin C, while garlic is thought to have a role in the prevention of blood clots and thus in protection from heart disease.

Spanish-style green beans *judías verdes* In Spain, this dish is normally served as a separate course before the main course. Try substituting snow peas or sugar snap peas for the green beans to vary the dish.

INGREDIENTS *1 tablespoon white wine vinegar* ‖ *3 cups green beans, trimmed* ‖ *2 tablespoons olive oil* ‖ *1 small onion, finely chopped* ‖ *2 garlic cloves, finely chopped* ‖ *salt and freshly ground black pepper*

ONE Bring a saucepan of water to the boil, add the vinegar and green beans and cook for 3–4 minutes. Drain, refresh the beans under cold running water and drain again. Pat the beans dry with paper towels. **TWO** Heat the oil in a large, nonstick skillet, add the onion and beans and cook over a medium heat, stirring frequently, for 3–4 minutes. Add the garlic and cook, stirring, for an additional minute. **THREE** Season to taste with salt and pepper, then reduce the heat, cover, and cook the beans over a very low heat for 5–6 minutes. Serve immediately.

Serves 4

NUTRIENT ANALYSIS PER SERVING 330 kJ – 80 cal – 2 g protein – 5 g carbohydrate – 3 g sugars – 6 g fat – 1 g saturated fat – 8 g fiber – 1 mg sodium

HEALTHY TIP Green beans and snow peas both contain good amounts of carotene, which in the body becomes vitamin A, an important antioxidant. Both vegetables are also sources of dietary fiber.

Spring vegetable stew

menestra de verduras Spring vegetables are used in this recipe from the Basque region to make a delectable, pretty, and very tasty one-pot vegetable meal.

INGREDIENTS *2 tablespoons olive oil* ‖ *4 oz baby onions or small shallots, peeled but left whole* ‖ *2 garlic cloves, finely chopped* ‖ *8 oz baby new potatoes, peeled and cooked until just tender* ‖ *8 oz baby carrots, trimmed and halved or quartered if large* ‖ *1½ cups shelled fresh or frozen fava beans* ‖ *2 tablespoons half-fat crème fraîche or sour cream* ‖ *salt and freshly ground black pepper* ‖ *green onions, sliced, to garnish*

ONE Heat the oil in a large skillet. Add the baby onions or shallots and garlic, cover, and cook over a low heat, stirring occasionally, for 10–12 minutes until the onions or shallots are soft. Add the potatoes and cook over a medium-low heat, stirring frequently, for 3–4 minutes. Remove from the heat, cover, and keep warm. **TWO** Bring a saucepan of lightly salted water to a boil, add the carrots and cook for 6–8 minutes or until just tender. Add the fava beans and cook for 2–3 minutes. Drain and transfer to the onion or shallot and potato mixture. **THREE** Add the crème fraîche or sour cream, season to taste with salt and pepper and toss to combine. Return to the heat and cook over a high heat, stirring, for 2–3 minutes. Serve immediately, garnished with the sliced green onions.

Serves 4

NUTRIENT ANALYSIS PER SERVING 753 kJ – 180 cal – 6 g protein – 20 g carbohydrate – 7 g sugars – 9 g fat – 2 g saturated fat – 3 g fiber – 46 mg sodium

HEALTHY TIP To preserve the vitamin content of all the vegetables in this recipe, try to prepare them as close to cooking time as possible.

Fava beans with ham *habas con jamón*

Fava beans are grown all over the Balearics and Catalonia, often planted between the olive trees. The sweetness of young fava beans marries perfectly with the Serrano ham.

INGREDIENTS *1 lb 10 oz fresh fava beans in their pods* ‖ *2–3 tablespoons olive oil* ‖ *2 garlic cloves, thinly sliced* ‖ *1 small onion, finely chopped* ‖ *4 tablespoons finely chopped Serrano ham* ‖ *¾ cup fino sherry* ‖ *¾ cup water* ‖ *1 teaspoon finely chopped marjoram leaves* ‖ *2 hard-cooked eggs, shelled and finely chopped* ‖ *salt and freshly ground black pepper*

ONE Remove the beans from their pods. Heat the oil in a large, heavy saucepan, add the garlic, onion, and ham and cook, stirring, for 3–4 minutes. Add the beans, sherry, measurement water, and marjoram, season to taste with salt and pepper, and bring to a boil. Reduce the heat to low, cover, and simmer gently for 1 hour or until the beans are tender. **TWO** Uncover the pan and cook to evaporate the remaining liquid (the mixture should be moist, but not too liquid). **THREE** Transfer to a warmed serving dish and sprinkle with the eggs. Serve immediately.

Serves 4

NUTRIENT ANALYSIS PER SERVING 1090 kJ – 260 cal – 14 g protein – 9 g carbohydrate – 3 g sugars – 13 g fat – 3 g saturated fat – 4 g fiber – 348 mg sodium

HEALTHY TIP Fava beans are a great source of dietary fiber and contain quite high levels of carotene, the vitamin A precursor. Take care to cook fava beans properly, because the inner part of the bean can, if eaten raw, cause a form of anemia in some people.

Catalan-style spinach

espinacas Catalanas Fresh spinach is cooked quickly with golden raisins and pine nuts in this typical Catalan dish, which is wonderful served with grilled or toasted crusty bread.

INGREDIENTS *⅓ cup golden raisins ‖ 1 lb 10 oz spinach, roughly chopped ‖ 2 tablespoons olive oil ‖ 2 garlic cloves, finely chopped ‖ 1 onion, finely chopped ‖ 4 tablespoons pine nuts, lightly toasted ‖ salt and freshly ground black pepper*

ONE Soak the raisins in a bowl of hot water for 20 minutes to plump up. Drain and set aside. **TWO** Bring a large saucepan of water to a boil, add the spinach and cook for 2–3 minutes. Drain and squeeze out the excess liquid. **THREE** Heat the oil in a large, nonstick skillet, add the garlic and onion and cook over a medium heat, stirring, for 4–5 minutes. **FOUR** Add the drained spinach, raisins, and pine nuts to the pan, season to taste with salt and pepper and cook, stirring, for 2–3 minutes or until warmed through. Serve immediately.

Serves 4

NUTRIENT ANALYSIS PER SERVING 868 kJ – 209 cal – 8 g protein – 14 g carbohydrate – 13 g sugars – 14 g fat – 1 g saturated fat – 9 g fiber – 283 mg sodium

HEALTHY TIP Spinach is a helpful source of folic acid (which tends to occur in dark green leafy vegetables). Pine nuts are rich in the antioxidant vitamin E, while golden raisins contain the energy-boosting minerals iron and potassium.

Aromatic dressed artichokes *alcachofas en vinagreta aromática*

If you are unable to find fresh artichokes for this dish, use top-quality bottled or canned artichoke hearts, drain well and pat dry with paper towels before pouring over the spiced dressing.

INGREDIENTS *4 globe artichokes* ‖ *2 garlic cloves, crushed* ‖ *1 teaspoon ground cumin* ‖ *1 teaspoon ground coriander* ‖ *½ teaspoon crushed red pepper* ‖ *1 tablespoon finely chopped oregano leaves* ‖ *2 tablespoons sherry vinegar* ‖ *2 tablespoons store-bought or homemade Vegetable Stock (see page 16)* ‖ *4 tablespoons olive oil* ‖ *salt and freshly ground black pepper* ‖ *finely chopped flat leaf parsley, to garnish*

ONE Trim the artichokes, cutting off the stalks to within 2 inches of the base, and remove and discard the tough outer leaves. Cut off the top quarter of the leaves from each artichoke and cut each one lengthwise in half or in quarters if large. **TWO** Using a teaspoon, scoop out and discard the hairy "choke" from the center of the artichoke sections and put in a bowl of water with a little lemon juice added to prevent discoloration. **THREE** Bring a large saucepan of lightly salted water to a boil, add the artichokes and return to a boil. Reduce the heat and simmer gently for 20–25 minutes or until tender. Remove with a slotted spoon, drain, cut-side down, on paper towels and allow to cool. **FOUR** Meanwhile, to make the dressing, mix the garlic, cumin, coriander, crushed pepper, oregano, vinegar, stock, and oil together in a bowl until well combined and season to taste with salt and pepper. **FIVE** Arrange the artichokes in a shallow serving dish in a single layer. Pour over the dressing, cover, and allow to stand at room temperature for 15–20 minutes before serving, garnished with chopped parsley.

Serves 4 as a tapa

NUTRIENT ANALYSIS PER SERVING 466 kJ – 113 cal – 2 g protein – 2 g carbohydrate – 1 g sugars – 11 g fat – 2 g saturated fat – 1 g fiber – 16 mg sodium

HEALTHY TIP Artichokes are a good source of some minerals and trace minerals, including phosphorus, magnesium, manganese, and chromium. They also contain cynarin and sylmarin, which are thought to help the liver regenerate healthy tissue.

Roasted vegetable salad *escalivada* Escaliver means to cook over hot embers.

In this Catalan dish, a colorful selection of classic Mediterranean vegetables are roasted in the oven and then tossed with a cumin- and rosemary-flavored dressing. Serve with crusty bread.

INGREDIENTS *2 onions, cut into thick wedges* ‖ *1 eggplant, cut into thick slices* ‖ *1 red sweet pepper, cored, seeded, and thickly sliced* ‖ *1 yellow sweet pepper, cored, seeded, and thickly sliced* ‖ *2 tomatoes, cut into thick wedges* ‖ *8 garlic cloves in their skins* ‖ *olive oil, for drizzling* ‖ *salt and freshly ground pepper*

DRESSING *2 teaspoons cumin seeds* ‖ *2 tablespoons lemon juice* ‖ *3 tablespoons sherry vinegar* ‖ *4 tablespoons olive oil* ‖ *1 teaspoon pimentón dulce (mild paprika)* ‖ *1 teaspoon finely chopped rosemary leaves*

ONE Spread all the vegetables and garlic out over 2 baking sheets and lightly drizzle with oil. Roast in a preheated oven, 375°F, for 25–30 minutes. **TWO** Remove from the oven and, when cool enough to handle, slip the garlic cloves from their skins into a blender or food processor. Add all the dressing ingredients and blend until smooth. **THREE** Arrange the vegetables in a serving dish and pour over the dressing. Toss to mix well, season to taste with salt and pepper and serve warm or at room temperature.

Serves 4 as a tapa

NUTRIENT ANALYSIS PER SERVING 812 kJ – 195 cal – 4 g protein – 16 g carbohydrate – 13 g sugars – 14 g fat – 2 g saturated fat – 6 g fiber – 17 mg sodium

HEALTHY TIP Onions and garlic are both thought to help prevent blood clots and preserve a healthy heart. Red and yellow sweet peppers are particularly high in vitamin C and carotene (which the body converts to vitamin A) and therefore have powerful antioxidant properties.

Chickpeas with Swiss chard

garbanzos con grelos The nutritious chickpea is a highly versatile legume and it is also very inexpensive. Here it is teamed with tender Swiss chard, but you can use any other leafy greens instead in this recipe. If you are short of time, use a 13 oz can of chickpeas instead of preparing chickpeas from dried.

INGREDIENTS *1½ cups dried chickpeas* ‖ *3 cups water* ‖ *1 large carrot, cut into small dice* ‖ *1 flat leaf parsley sprig* ‖ *1 bay leaf* ‖ *1 large onion, chopped* ‖ *2 tablespoons olive oil* ‖ *2 garlic cloves, chopped* ‖ *1 red onion, finely chopped* ‖ *2 ripe tomatoes, roughly chopped* ‖ *8 oz Swiss chard, roughly chopped* ‖ *salt and freshly ground black pepper*

ONE Soak the chickpeas in plenty of cold water overnight. Drain, rinse, and put in a large saucepan with the measurement water, carrot, parsley sprig, bay leaf, and onion. Bring to a boil, skimming off any foam that rises to the surface, then reduce the heat and simmer, uncovered, for 20–25 minutes or until tender.

TWO Meanwhile, heat the oil in a skillet, add the garlic and red onion and cook over a medium heat, stirring, for 3–4 minutes. Increase the heat, add the tomatoes and cook, stirring frequently, for 5–6 minutes.

THREE Add the tomato mixture to the pan of chickpeas and stir in the Swiss chard. Only season to taste with salt and pepper now (the chickpeas will not soften if salt is added before they are tender) and bring to a boil. Reduce the heat and simmer gently, uncovered, for 5–6 minutes. Transfer to a warmed serving bowl.

Serves 4

NUTRIENT ANALYSIS PER SERVING 1344 kJ – 319 cal – 16 g protein – 45 g carbohydrate – 12 g sugars – 10 g fat – 1 g saturated fat – 12 g fiber – 170 mg sodium

HEALTHY TIP Chickpeas are highly nutritious, providing useful amounts of protein, carbohydrate, iron, and fiber. Swiss chard contains some carotene, vitamin C, and folic acid, in addition to small quantities of the B vitamins and trace minerals.

Griddled asparagus with lemon mayonnaise *espárragos con salsa mayonesa*

This Andalusian recipe is a wonderfully simple treatment of a delicate vegetable. If you can, try to find wild asparagus in the spring. This recipe uses a reduced-fat mayonnaise, flavored with lemon, to accompany the green beauties in healthy style.

INGREDIENTS *1 lb 10 oz asparagus spears, trimmed and bases peeled* ‖ *3 tablespoons olive oil* ‖ *salt and freshly ground black pepper*

LEMON MAYONNAISE *¾ cup reduced-fat mayonnaise* ‖ *2 garlic cloves, crushed* ‖ *2 teaspoons finely grated lemon zest* ‖ *2 tablespoons lemon juice* ‖ *pinch of pimentón dulce (mild paprika)*

ONE Arrange the asparagus in a shallow dish in a single layer. Drizzle over the oil and season to taste with salt and pepper. Gently turn the asparagus to coat evenly with the oil. **TWO** To make the lemon mayonnaise, beat all the ingredients together in a small bowl and season to taste with salt and pepper. Cover and set aside. **THREE** Heat a large, heavy griddle pan over a high heat until smoking. Add the asparagus, in batches, and cook for 2–3 minutes on each side or until lightly charred at the edges. Remove from the pan and keep hot while cooking the remaining asparagus. Serve hot with the lemon mayonnaise.

Serves 4

NUTRIENT ANALYSIS PER SERVING 1107 kJ – 268 cal – 6 g protein – 8 g carbohydrate – 6 g sugars – 24 g fat – 1 g saturated fat – 3 g fiber – 470 mg sodium

HEALTHY TIP Asparagus is a good source of folic acid and of the vitamin A precursor, carotene. Cook the asparagus for as short a time as possible to minimize loss of folic acid in cooking.

Eggplant and mixed vegetable stew *pisto Manchego* From the

region of La Mancha in central Spain comes this flavorful dish of eggplants cooked with zucchini, sweet peppers, and tomatoes. Sometimes it is topped with a fried or poached egg and it is equally good served at room temperature with some good bread and a slice of Manchego cheese.

INGREDIENTS *2 tablespoons olive oil* ‖ *3 garlic cloves, crushed* ‖ *1 onion, finely chopped* ‖ *2 eggplants, cut into ½ inch dice* ‖ *2 zucchini, cut into ½ inch dice* ‖ *2 red sweet peppers, cored, seeded, and cut into ½ inch pieces* ‖ *13 oz can chopped tomatoes* ‖ *1 teaspoon pimentón dulce (mild paprika)* ‖ *1 teaspoon golden superfine sugar* ‖ *1 tablespoon roughly chopped oregano leaves, plus extra whole leaves to garnish* ‖ *2 teaspoons sherry vinegar* ‖ *salt and freshly ground black pepper* ‖ *4 poached eggs, to serve (optional)*

ONE Heat the oil in a large skillet, add the garlic and onion and cook over a medium heat, stirring frequently, for 6–8 minutes. **TWO** Increase the heat to high, add the eggplants and cook, stirring, for 4–5 minutes. Add the zucchini and sweet peppers and cook, stirring, for 3–4 minutes. **THREE** Stir in the tomatoes and their juice, *pimentón*, sugar, oregano, and vinegar, season to taste with salt and pepper and bring to a boil. Reduce the heat, cover tightly, and simmer gently for 20–25 minutes. **FOUR** Remove from the heat and allow to stand for 10 minutes before serving. Serve each portion with a poached egg, if you desire, and sprinkle with some oregano leaves to garnish.

Serves 4

NUTRIENT ANALYSIS PER SERVING 634 kJ – 150 cal – 5 g protein – 19 g carbohydrate – 14 g sugars – 7 g fat – 1 g saturated fat – 7 g fiber – 48 mg sodium

HEALTHY TIP Eggplants contain only small amounts of most vitamins, but the tomatoes, peppers, and zucchini in this dish add plenty of vitamin C and other antioxidants.

Sautéed mushrooms with parsley and garlic *setas salteadas*

For this recipe you can use any large, fleshy mushrooms that you can find, such as field or Portobello mushrooms. Usually served as a first course in Spain, this also makes a great accompaniment to chicken and meat dishes. Serve with crusty bread if using as an appetizer.

INGREDIENTS *1 lb large mushrooms, trimmed* ‖ *4 tablespoons olive oil* ‖ *3 garlic cloves, finely chopped* ‖ *4 tablespoons finely chopped flat leaf parsley* ‖ *3 tablespoons fresh white bread crumbs* ‖ *salt and freshly ground black pepper*

ONE Cut the mushrooms in half or quarters, or thinly slice them. Heat the oil in a large skillet, add the mushrooms, garlic, and parsley and cook over a medium heat, stirring frequently, for 6–8 minutes or until the mushrooms are lightly browned and have released all their liquid. **TWO** Stir in the bread crumbs, season to taste with salt and pepper and stir to mix. Serve immediately.

Serves 4

NUTRIENT ANALYSIS PER SERVING 615 kJ – 148 cal – 4 g protein – 7 g carbohydrate – 1 g sugars – 12 g fat – 2 g saturated fat – 4 g fiber – 73 mg sodium

HEALTHY TIP Mushrooms provide potassium, which regulates blood pressure and helps the body beat fatigue. Some types of mushroom are considered capable of warding off viruses and combating allergies.

Spinach, tomato, and pine nut flatbread _coca d'espinacas_

A typical bread from the Balearic region, this can be topped with a variety of different ingredients of your choice and made into any shape that you desire.

INGREDIENTS _1 cup plus 1½ tablespoons white bread flour, plus extra for dusting_ ‖ _scant ¼ oz envelope of quick-rising active dry yeast_ ‖ _1 tablespoon very finely chopped rosemary_ ‖ _1 teaspoon sea salt_ ‖ _2 teaspoons olive oil, plus extra for oiling and drizzling_ ‖ _½ cup hand-hot water_ ‖ _freshly ground black pepper_

TOPPING _2 cups baby spinach leaves, roughly chopped_ ‖ _1 small onion, halved and very thinly sliced_ ‖ _2 garlic cloves, thinly sliced_ ‖ _15 small cherry tomatoes, about 7 oz_ ‖ _1 tablespoon pine nuts_

ONE Put the flour in a bowl with the yeast, rosemary, and salt. Season to taste with pepper. Make a well in the center and pour in the oil and the measurement hand-hot water. Using your fingers, mix the wet ingredients into the dry until a dough forms and comes away from the side of the bowl, adding a little extra water if the mixture seems too dry. **TWO** Transfer the dough to a lightly floured work surface and knead for 6–8 minutes. Form the dough into a ball. Put the dough in a lightly oiled bowl, cover and set aside in a warm place for 1 hour or until almost doubled in size. **THREE** Turn out the dough onto a floured work surface and flatten. Roll out with a rolling pin to a rectangle about 10 x 8 inches and ½ inch thick. Transfer to a nonstick baking sheet. **FOUR** Spread the dough with the spinach and sprinkle with the onion, garlic, and tomatoes. Drizzle over a little oil, season to taste with salt and pepper and sprinkle with the pine nuts. **FIVE** Bake in a preheated oven, 425°F, for 12–15 minutes or until the bread is slightly risen and golden. Cut into rectangles and serve warm or at room temperature.

Serves 4

NUTRIENT ANALYSIS PER SERVING 765 kJ – 180 cal – 6 g protein – 32 g carbohydrate – 3 g sugars – 4 g fat – 1 g saturated fat – 4 g fiber – 534 mg sodium

HEALTHY TIP This flatbread is high in most nutrients and has a low fat content. Cherry tomatoes are a great source of vitamin C and carotene, and they also have a higher fiber content than larger tomatoes, because of the increased ratio of skin to flesh.

Meat and poultry

Quails with pine nuts and golden raisins *codorniz con pasas de esmirna y piñones* These dainty little birds team well with the Roasted Vegetable Salad *(see page 90)* and steamed green vegetables of your choice.

INGREDIENTS *⅓ cup golden raisins* ‖ *2 quails, 5–7 oz each* ‖ *3 tablespoons olive oil* ‖ *¼ cup pine nuts* ‖ *3 tablespoons fino sherry* ‖ *salt and freshly ground black pepper*

ONE Soak the raisins in a bowl of hot water for about 1 hour to plump up. **TWO** Meanwhile, arrange the quails on a baking sheet and rub 2 tablespoons of the oil all over them. Season to taste with salt and pepper and roast in a preheated oven, 375°F, for 15–20 minutes or until cooked through, tender and golden. Remove from the oven and transfer to a warmed serving dish. Cover with foil and leave to rest in a warm place while you finish preparing the dish. **THREE** Heat the remaining oil in a small skillet. Drain the raisins, add to the pan with the pine nuts and cook, stirring, for 2–3 minutes. Add the sherry and cook, stirring, for 1 minute. Spoon the mixture over the quails and serve immediately.

Serves 2

NUTRIENT ANALYSIS PER SERVING 2044 kJ – 490 cal – 30 g protein – 18 g carbohydrate – 18 g sugars – 31 g fat – 4 g saturated fat – 2 g fiber – 80 mg sodium

HEALTHY TIP Like most nuts, pine nuts are a good source of the antioxidant vitamin E. There is some evidence that vitamin E may be protective against heart disease and cancers.

Chicken with orange and mint *pollo a la naranja y menta*

Mint leaves and freshly squeezed orange juice flavor this chicken dish, which makes a special supper when served with sautéed potatoes and a salad, such as the Broiled Red Pepper Salad *(see page 68)* or Rice and Olive Salad *(see page 66)*.

INGREDIENTS *4 boneless, skinless chicken breasts, about 7 oz each* ‖ *3 tablespoons olive oil* ‖ *⅔ cup freshly squeezed orange juice* ‖ *2 tablespoons chopped mint leaves, plus extra to garnish* ‖ *1 tablespoon butter* ‖ *salt and freshly ground black pepper* ‖ *orange slices, to garnish*

ONE Season the chicken breasts to taste with salt and pepper. Heat the oil in a large, nonstick skillet, add the chicken breasts and cook over a medium heat, turning once, for 4–5 minutes or until golden all over. **TWO** Pour in the orange juice and bring to a simmer. Cover tightly, reduce the heat to low and cook gently for 8–10 minutes. **THREE** Add the chopped mint and butter and stir to mix well. Cook over a high heat, stirring, for 2 minutes. **FOUR** Serve the chicken immediately, garnished with chopped mint leaves and the orange slices.

Serves 4

NUTRIENT ANALYSIS PER SERVING 1454 kJ – 347 cal – 44 g protein – 3 g carbohydrate – 3 g sugars – 18 g fat – 5 g saturated fat – 0 g fiber – 173 mg sodium

HEALTHY TIP Orange juice is a good source of vitamin C, although some will be lost in the cooking process as the vitamin is heat-sensitive. To reduce the salt in the recipe, use unsalted or slightly salted butter.

Chicken and chickpea stew *cocido Madrileño* A *cocido* is a one-pot

dish that is always based on legumes. This hearty chickpea and chicken example originates from Madrid and is usually eaten as a midday meal.

INGREDIENTS *2 cups dried chickpeas* ‖ *3 lb skinless chicken leg joints* ‖ *8 cups water* ‖ *1 whole head of garlic* ‖ *4 oz Serrano ham, chopped* ‖ *1 tablespoon pimentón dulce (mild paprika)* ‖ *1 large onion, roughly chopped* ‖ *2 large carrots, roughly chopped* ‖ *4 celery sticks, roughly chopped* ‖ *1 cup finely shredded green cabbage* ‖ *salt and freshly ground black pepper*

ONE Soak the chickpeas in plenty of cold water overnight. Drain, rinse, and put in a large, heavy saucepan with the chicken and measurement water. Bring to a boil, skimming off any foam that rises to the surface. **TWO** Add all the remaining ingredients, except the cabbage, and return to a boil. Reduce the heat to low, cover tightly, and simmer gently for 1½ hours. The chickpeas should be tender and the chicken almost falling off the bone. **THREE** Only season to taste with salt and pepper now (the chickpeas will not soften if salt is added before they are tender) and add the cabbage. Bring to a boil and cook for 6–8 minutes. Ladle into warmed bowls and serve immediately.

Serves 4

NUTRIENT ANALYSIS PER SERVING 2419 kJ – 575 cal – 56 g protein – 54 g carbohydrate – 10 g sugars – 17 g fat – 4 g saturated fat – 15 g fiber – 700 mg sodium

HEALTHY TIP Chickpeas are high in iron and dietary fiber and they are also a good source of protein. Carrots are useful for the betacarotenes they contain, which the body uses to make vitamin A. This vitamin is, among other things, essential for good vision.

Lamb with lemon and garlic *cochifrito* This simple and delicious lamb

stew is from the Aragon region of northeastern Spain. The lemon juice brings out the full flavor of the lamb, which is further enhanced by the addition of garlic and fresh parsley. Serve with Catalan-style Spinach *(see page 86)*.

INGREDIENTS *1¾ lb lean boneless lamb, cut into bite-size pieces* ‖ *2 tablespoons olive oil* ‖ *4 garlic cloves, crushed* ‖ *1 onion, finely chopped* ‖ *1 tablespoon pimentón dulce (mild paprika)* ‖ *3 tablespoons lemon juice* ‖ *4 tablespoons finely chopped flat leaf parsley, plus extra to garnish* ‖ *½ cup store-bought or homemade Vegetable or Chicken Stock (see pages 16–17)* ‖ *salt and freshly ground black pepper* ‖ *finely grated lemon zest, to garnish*

ONE Season the lamb to taste with salt and pepper. Heat the oil in a large, nonstick skillet over a medium-high heat, add the lamb and cook, turning frequently, for 6–8 minutes until the meat is browned all over.

TWO Transfer to a heavy, flameproof casserole and add the garlic, onion, *pimentón*, lemon juice, parsley, and stock. Cover tightly and simmer gently over a low heat for 1½ hours or until the lamb is tender. Serve immediately, garnished with finely chopped parsley and grated lemon zest.

Serves 4

NUTRIENT ANALYSIS PER SERVING 1779 kJ – 425 cal – 47 g protein – 4 g carbohydrate – 2 g sugars – 25 g fat – 10 g saturated fat – 1 g fiber – 196 mg sodium

HEALTHY TIP Lamb can be quite high in fat, depending on the cut of the meat. To keep down the fat content of this dish, use lean leg meat and cut off any visible fat.

Stuffed roasted chicken *pollo relleno* This dish makes a great centerpiece

for a Sunday lunch when served with mashed potatoes and a green or mixed salad. Or try serving it with the Sautéed Mushrooms *(see page 96)* or Griddled Asparagus *(see page 94)*. Choose a corn-fed chicken for the most delicious results.

INGREDIENTS *1 whole chicken, about 3 lb* ‖ *olive oil, for brushing* ‖ *salt and freshly ground black pepper*

STUFFING *4 oz chorizo sausage, chopped* ‖ *4 oz lean ground pork* ‖ *4 tablespoons chopped flat leaf parsley* ‖ *4 garlic cloves, crushed* ‖ *pinch of ground nutmeg* ‖ *2 tablespoons finely chopped onion* ‖ *1 tablespoon chopped oregano leaves* ‖ *finely grated zest and juice of 1 lemon* ‖ *1 egg, beaten*

ONE To make the stuffing, put all the ingredients in a bowl, season to taste with salt and pepper and, using your fingers, mix together until they are well combined. **TWO** Push the stuffing into the body cavity of the chicken and tie the legs together with fine kitchen string. Transfer the chicken to a roasting pan, lightly brush with oil and season to taste with salt and pepper. **THREE** Roast in a preheated oven, 400°F, for 30 minutes. Reduce the oven temperature to 325°F, and roast for an additional 30–35 minutes or until the juices run clear when the chicken is pierced between the thigh and body. **FOUR** Remove from the oven, cover with foil and leave to rest in a warm place for 10–15 minutes. Carve and serve a little stuffing with each portion of chicken.

Serves 4

NUTRIENT ANALYSIS PER SERVING 2620 kJ – 630 cal – 58 g protein – 3 g carbohydrate – 2 g sugars – 43 g fat – 13 g saturated fat – 1 g fiber – 350 mg sodium

HEALTHY TIP Most of the fat in a chicken is stored in the skin. To reduce the fat content of the dish, pour away any fat that collects in the roasting dish during the cooking process.

Basque-style duck *pato a la vasca* Basque cooking is renowned for its excellence

and often produces the simplest and most delicious Spanish food. This dish is a prime example.

INGREDIENTS *1 teaspoon pimentón dulce (mild paprika)* ‖ *pinch of ground cloves* ‖ *1 teaspoon ground cinnamon* ‖ *4 large duck breasts, about 9 oz each* ‖ *3 tablespoons olive oil* ‖ *6 green onions, finely chopped* ‖ *2 garlic cloves, crushed* ‖ *2 tablespoons all-purpose flour* ‖ *½ cup sweet sherry* ‖ *¾ cup store-bought or homemade Chicken Stock (see page 17)* ‖ *4 tablespoons finely chopped tarragon, plus a sprig to garnish* ‖ *1 thyme sprig* ‖ *salt and freshly ground black pepper*

ONE Rub the spices over the duck, and season with salt and pepper. **TWO** Heat a large skillet over a high heat, then add the oil and heat. Add the duck and cook for 2–3 minutes on each side until lightly browned. Transfer to a baking sheet with a slotted spoon. Roast in a preheated oven, 350°F, for 15–20 minutes. **THREE** Meanwhile, heat the skillet, add the green onions and garlic and cook, stirring, for 1–2 minutes. Add the flour and cook, stirring constantly, for 30–40 seconds. Pour in the sherry and cook for 1–2 minutes, then add the stock. Bring to a boil, stirring, then reduce the heat and add the herbs. Simmer for 4–5 minutes. **FOUR** Remove the duck from the oven and add to the pan. Toss to coat with the sauce, adjust the seasoning, and serve immediately, garnished with a sprig of tarragon.

Serves 4

NUTRIENT ANALYSIS PER SERVING 1069 kJ – 256 cal – 17 g protein – 11 g carbohydrate – 2 g sugars – 14 g fat – 3 g saturated fat – 0 g fiber – 90 mg sodium

HEALTHY TIP Duck is quite high in fat, but much of this is in the skin or just under it and will run out in the roasting process. Use a slotted spoon to transfer the duck, to allow as much of the fat as possible to be poured away.

Madrid-style pork

lomo a la Madrileña In this easy recipe, lean pork tenderloin is marinated with herbs and spices and then simply grilled. Serve with steamed greens or the Spanish-style Green Beans *(see page 81)* and boiled potatoes.

INGREDIENTS *3 garlic cloves, crushed* ‖ *1 tablespoon pimentón dulce (mild paprika)* ‖ *1 teaspoon dried oregano* ‖ *1 teaspoon chopped thyme leaves* ‖ *2 tablespoons olive oil* ‖ *1 lb pork tenderloin* ‖ *salt and freshly ground black pepper*

ONE Mix the garlic, *pimentón*, oregano, thyme, and oil together in a small bowl and season to taste with salt and pepper. **TWO** Put the pork in a shallow dish and rub the herb and spice mixture all over. Cover with plastic wrap and allow to marinate overnight in the refrigerator, turning the pork occasionally. **THREE** When ready to cook, remove the pork from the refrigerator and allow to return to room temperature. Slice the pork into ¾ inch thick rounds. **FOUR** Heat a griddle pan over a high heat until smoking, add the pork, in batches, and cook for 2–3 minutes on each side or until cooked to your liking, but do not overcook. Remove from the pan and keep warm while cooking the remaining pork. Serve hot.

Serves 4

NUTRIENT ANALYSIS PER SERVING 987 kJ – 237 cal – 26 g protein – 1 g carbohydrate – 0 g sugars – 15 g fat – 4 g saturated fat – 0 g fiber – 70 mg sodium

HEALTHY TIP Although there is some fat running through the meat, giving it texture and flavor, pork is a leaner meat today than in the past. Choose a lean cut and remove any visible fat.

Chicken with red peppers

pollo chilindrón This chicken dish originally came from Aragon in northeastern Spain, but can now be found all over the country—a testament to just how delicious and popular it is! Serve it with boiled rice or mashed potatoes, together with Garlicky Cauliflower *(see page 80)*.

INGREDIENTS *4 tablespoons olive oil* ‖ *2 lb skinless chicken thighs* ‖ *4 garlic cloves, crushed* ‖ *1 onion, finely chopped* ‖ *2 oz Serrano ham, diced* ‖ *3 red sweet peppers, cored, seeded, and thinly sliced* ‖ *13 oz can chopped tomatoes* ‖ *1 thyme sprig* ‖ *1 bay leaf* ‖ *salt and freshly ground black pepper* ‖ *chopped flat leaf parsley, to garnish*

ONE Heat the oil in a large, heavy, shallow flameproof casserole, add the chicken, garlic, and onion and cook them over a medium heat, turning frequently, for 4–5 minutes until the chicken is golden all over. **TWO** Add the ham and sweet peppers and cook, stirring, for 1–2 minutes. **THREE** Add the tomatoes and their juice, thyme sprig, and bay leaf and bring to a boil. Reduce the heat to very low, cover tightly, and cook for 1½ hours until the chicken is meltingly tender. **FOUR** Season to taste with salt and pepper, garnish with chopped parsley and serve.

Serves 4

NUTRIENT ANALYSIS PER SERVING 1535 kJ – 368 cal – 34 g protein – 10 g carbohydrate – 9 g sugars – 21 g fat – 5 g saturated fat – 3 g fiber – 427 mg sodium

HEALTHY TIP The addition of Serrano ham to the chicken increases the sodium content of this dish. Taste the sauce before adding any extra salt.

Valencian paella

paella Valenciana This typical Spanish midday dish has for its main ingredients rice, saffron, and water. The remainder can be whatever comes to hand. This simplified version features chicken and chorizo, but shrimp, mussels, clams, and even snails are other favorite additions.

INGREDIENTS *2 lb skinless chicken thighs, cut into large pieces ‖ 4 tablespoons olive oil ‖ 7 oz chorizo sausage, cut into ¼ inch slices ‖ 2 onions, finely chopped ‖ 4 garlic cloves, chopped ‖ 2 red sweet peppers, cored, seeded, and finely chopped ‖ 3½ cups paella rice, such as Calasparra or Bomba ‖ 3 tablespoons finely chopped flat leaf parsley, plus extra to garnish ‖ 1 bay leaf ‖ a large pinch of saffron threads ‖ 6 cups store-bought or homemade Chicken Stock (see page 17) ‖ ⅔ cup fresh or frozen peas ‖ ½ cup shelled fresh or frozen fava beans ‖ salt and freshly ground black pepper*

ONE Pat the chicken dry with paper towels and season to taste with salt and pepper. Heat the oil in a *paellera* or a heavy, shallow flameproof casserole over a medium-high heat, add the chicken and cook, turning frequently, for 4–5 minutes until it is golden all over. Remove with a slotted spoon to a plate and keep warm. **TWO** Add the chorizo to the pan with the onions, garlic, and red peppers and cook, stirring frequently, for 4–5 minutes. **THREE** Return the chicken and any juices that have accumulated to the pan and stir in the rice, parsley, bay leaf, and saffron. Stir in the stock, peas, and fava beans, bring to a simmer and cook over a low heat, uncovered, for 12–15 minutes. **FOUR** Reduce the heat to very low, cover tightly and cook for an additional 12–15 minutes until the rice is tender and all the liquid has been absorbed. **FIVE** Remove the pan from the heat and allow to stand, covered, for 10 minutes before serving the paella, garnished with chopped parsley.

Serves 6–8

NUTRIENT ANALYSIS PER SERVING 3145 kJ – 746 cal – 33 g protein – 113 g carbohydrate – 7 g sugars – 21 g fat – 6 g saturated fat – 5 g fiber – 277 mg sodium

HEALTHY TIP Rice and meat are combined to make a nutritious dish, high in protein and quite low in fat. Fava beans and peas are great sources of fiber, and peppers and onions provide protective antioxidants.

Rabbit with wild mushrooms *conejo con setas silvestres* Rabbit

is a popular ingredient in Spanish cooking, as are mushrooms harvested from the countryside—usually flat, brown mushrooms called *rovellones*. Cooked in full-bodied red wine, they make a memorable duo in this rich stew. Serve with hot mashed potatoes and carrots, or try serving it with the Spring Vegetable Stew *(see page 82)*.

INGREDIENTS *3 tablespoons olive oil* ‖ *2 lb whole rabbit, cut into large pieces* ‖ *2 onions, finely chopped* ‖ *4 garlic cloves, finely chopped* ‖ *7 oz Serrano ham, sliced* ‖ *1¼ cups Rioja or other robust red wine* ‖ *8 oz wild mushrooms, thickly sliced* ‖ *salt and freshly ground black pepper* ‖ *parsley, finely chopped, to garnish*

ONE Heat the oil in a large, flameproof casserole over a medium-high heat, add the rabbit and cook, turning frequently, for 4–5 minutes until browned all over. Remove with a slotted spoon to a plate and keep warm. **TWO** Add the onions and garlic to the casserole and cook over a low heat, stirring frequently, for 5–6 minutes until the onions are softened. **THREE** Increase the heat to high, add the ham and cook, stirring, for 3–4 minutes. Return the rabbit and any juices that have accumulated to the casserole. Pour over the wine, season to taste with salt and pepper and bring to a boil. Reduce the heat to low, cover tightly, and cook for 40 minutes. **FOUR** Add the mushrooms and stir to mix well. Re-cover and cook for an additional 12–15 minutes. Serve immediately, garnished with the parsley.

Serves 4

NUTRIENT ANALYSIS PER SERVING 1943 kJ – 319 cal – 50 g protein – 7 g carbohydrate – 5 g sugars – 21 g fat – 6 g saturated fat – 3 g fiber – 1117 mg sodium

HEALTHY TIP Rabbit is low in fat. It used to be thought of as a cheap substitute for chicken, but is now accepted as a tasty meat in its own right. The Serrano ham increases the sodium content of the recipe considerably, so taste the sauce before seasoning with extra salt.

Baked eggs with chorizo, ham, and asparagus

huevos a la flamenca This well-known Andalusian dish, originating from Seville, is very colorful to look at and makes a welcome lunch or supper dish.

INGREDIENTS *2 tablespoons olive oil* ‖ *1 onion, finely chopped* ‖ *3 garlic cloves, finely chopped* ‖ *13 oz can chopped tomatoes* ‖ *1 teaspoon golden superfine sugar* ‖ *1 teaspoon pimentón dulce (mild paprika)* ‖ *2 canned pimientos, drained and cut into thick strips* ‖ *12 asparagus tips* ‖ *⅔ cup fresh or frozen peas* ‖ *4 eggs* ‖ *4 oz chorizo sausage, roughly chopped* ‖ *4 oz Serrano ham, finely diced* ‖ *salt and freshly ground black pepper* ‖ *parsley, finely chopped, to garnish*

ONE Heat the oil in a large skillet, add the onion and garlic and cook over a medium heat, stirring frequently, for 10 minutes until the onion is soft. Add the tomatoes and their juice, sugar, and *pimentón* and cook over a high heat, stirring occasionally, for 10 minutes. Season to taste with salt and pepper, then transfer the mixture to a shallow, round ovenproof dish, about 10 inches in diameter. **TWO** Add the pimientos, asparagus, and peas and stir well. Make 4 indentations in the mixture and break an egg into each. **THREE** Bake in a preheated oven, 400°F, for 8–10 minutes or until the eggs are just set. Remove from the oven and keep warm. **FOUR** Heat a dry skillet until very hot, add the chorizo and ham and cook over a high heat, stirring, for 4–5 minutes until well browned and crisp. Spoon the chorizo and ham over the top of the vegetables and serve immediately, garnished with parsley.

Serves 4

NUTRIENT ANALYSIS PER SERVING 1330 kJ – 319 cal – 22 g protein – 15 g carbohydrate – 12 g sugars – 19 g fat – 5 g saturated fat – 5 g fiber – 740 mg sodium

HEALTHY TIP Eggs do contain cholesterol, but they are nutritious and can be safely eaten in moderation. Asparagus is a good source of folic acid, necessary for the formation of new cells in the body.

Lentils and chorizo stew *lentejas* Brown lentils are widely used in Spain in soups and salads as well as stews, such as this robust one, and they don't require any presoaking. This makes an easy, filling dish for entertaining. Serve with chunks of warm crusty bread.

INGREDIENTS *1¼ cups brown lentils, washed and drained* ‖ *1 leek, trimmed, cleaned, and thinly sliced* ‖ *2 onions, finely chopped* ‖ *2 carrots, finely diced* ‖ *2 garlic cloves, finely chopped* ‖ *8 oz chorizo sausage, finely chopped or sliced* ‖ *1 tablespoon pimentón dulce (mild paprika)* ‖ *2 tablespoons olive oil* ‖ *salt and freshly ground black pepper*

ONE Put the lentils in a large saucepan and cover with cold water (about 2 cups). Add the leek and one of the onions, the carrots, garlic, chorizo, and *pimentón* and season to taste with salt and pepper. Add half the oil and bring to a simmer. **TWO** Cover and cook over a very low heat for 45–50 minutes or until the lentils are tender. The mixture should be quite thick. **THREE** Meanwhile, heat the remaining oil in a small skillet, add the remaining onion and cook over a medium heat, stirring frequently, for 10–12 minutes until lightly browned. Stir into the lentil stew and serve immediately.

Serves 4

NUTRIENT ANALYSIS PER SERVING 1983 kJ – 473 cal – 28 g protein – 44 g carbohydrate – 11 g sugars – 22 g fat – 7 g saturated fat – 8 g fiber – 380 mg sodium

HEALTHY TIP Lentils are a good source of protein and also contain significant amounts of iron, which boosts the immune system and is essential for healthy blood.

Catalan-style noodles with pork sausages *fideos a la Catalana*

Fideus—*fideos* in Spanish—is short, thin Spanish pasta, very similar to Italian vermicelli, and was introduced to Catalonia by the Moors. In this dish, spicy fresh pork sausages are cooked with garlic, onions, and tomatoes to create a wonderfully hearty main course.

INGREDIENTS *4 tablespoons olive oil* ‖ *1¼ lb large fresh pork sausages* ‖ *1 large onion, finely chopped* ‖ *4 garlic cloves, finely chopped* ‖ *13 oz can tomatoes* ‖ *1 teaspoon pimentón dulce (mild paprika)* ‖ *8 oz fideus pasta or vermicelli, cut into short lengths* ‖ *4 cups store-bought or homemade Chicken or Vegetable Stock (see pages 16–17)* ‖ *salt and freshly ground black pepper* ‖ *chopped flat leaf parsley, to garnish*

ONE Heat half the oil in a 10 inch shallow flameproof casserole or skillet with a lid and an ovenproof handle. Add the sausages and cook over a medium-high heat, turning frequently, for 3–4 minutes or until lightly browned all over. Remove with a slotted spoon and set aside. **TWO** Heat the remaining oil in the pan, add the onion and garlic and cook over a low heat, stirring occasionally, for 10 minutes until soft. Add the tomatoes and their juice and *pimentón* and cook over a medium heat, stirring, for 3–4 minutes. Return the sausages to the pan with the pasta and stock. Season to taste with salt and pepper, stir to mix well and bring to a boil. **THREE** Cover the casserole or skillet and cook in a preheated oven, 375°C, for 20–25 minutes or until most of the liquid has been absorbed. **FOUR** Remove from the oven and sprinkle with the chopped parsley to garnish before serving straight from the casserole or pan.

Serves 4

NUTRIENT ANALYSIS PER SERVING 2814 kJ – 670 cal – 23 g protein – 66 g carbohydrate – 10 g sugars – 37 g fat – 11 g saturated fat – 6 g fiber – 1090 mg sodium

HEALTHY TIP Most sausages have quite a high salt content, so you won't need to add much salt to the pasta and stock during cooking. Combining meat with a starchy food such as pasta, potatoes, or rice improves the protein quality of the dish.

Fish and seafood

Spanish rice with clams and vegetables *arroz con almejas y vegetales*

Creamy rice and sweet clams are perfectly combined in this colorful dish, with the addition of plenty of fresh vegetables.

INGREDIENTS *4 tablespoons olive oil* ‖ *1 small red onion, finely chopped* ‖ *1 small leek, thinly sliced* ‖ *1 carrot, cut into ½ inch dice* ‖ *1 cup green beans, trimmed and cut into ½ inch lengths* ‖ *1 large tomato, skinned, seeded, and diced* ‖ *2 cups paella rice, such as Calasparra or Bomba* ‖ *2 garlic cloves, crushed* ‖ *20–25 live clams, prepared* (see page 14) ‖ *2 tablespoons tomato paste* ‖ *1 tablespoon pimentón dulce (mild paprika)* ‖ *⅔ cup dry white wine* ‖ *1 tablespoon chopped flat leaf parsley, plus extra to garnish* ‖ *salt and freshly ground black pepper*

ONE Heat half the oil in a large, nonstick skillet, add the onion, leek, carrot, and green beans and cook over a medium heat for 6–8 minutes until softened. Add the tomato and cook for 2–3 minutes. **TWO** Rinse the rice and drain. Add to the pan and cook, stirring, for 2–3 minutes. Add enough water to cover the rice and vegetables and slowly bring to a boil. **THREE** Meanwhile, heat the remaining oil in a saucepan, add the garlic and cook over a medium heat, stirring, for 1–2 minutes. Add the drained clams with the tomato paste, *pimentón*, wine, and parsley. Cover tightly and cook over a high heat, shaking the pan vigorously several times, for 4–5 minutes or until all the clams have opened (discard any that remain closed). **FOUR** Transfer the clams to the rice, mix well and cook for an additional 8–10 minutes or until the rice is just tender. Season with salt and pepper, garnish with chopped parsley, and serve immediately.

Serves 4

NUTRIENT ANALYSIS PER SERVING 2320 kJ – 550 cal – 13 g protein – 96 g carbohydrate – 6 g sugars – 13 g fat – 2 g saturated fat – 5 g fiber – 66 mg sodium

HEALTHY TIP As well as containing valuable omega-3 fatty acids, which are believed to have a protective effect against coronary heart disease, clams also provide minerals that are vital for wellbeing, such as iron, zinc, and selenium.

Griddled razor clams with a herb salsa *navajas con salsa*

verde Razor clams are quickly cooked in a griddle pan in this Basque recipe and served with a typical uncooked sauce from the region, *salsa verde*. Other shellfish such as mussels, clams, or even oysters can be used instead of the razor clams if desired.

INGREDIENTS *12 live razor shell clams, prepared* (*see page 14*)

SALSA VERDE *4 green onions, very finely chopped* ‖ *5 tablespoons finely chopped flat leaf parsley* ‖ *2 garlic cloves, crushed* ‖ *1 tablespoon sherry vinegar* ‖ *4 tablespoons olive oil* ‖ *1 teaspoon finely chopped green chili* ‖ *salt and freshly ground black pepper*

ONE To make the salsa, put all the ingredients in a blender or food processor, season to taste with salt and pepper and blend until well combined. Cover and set aside. **TWO** Heat a large, heavy griddle pan over a high heat until smoking. Add the drained clams and allow to cook in their own steam until they have all opened (discard any that remain closed). **THREE** Remove from the heat, then remove the clam meat from the shells. Cut into pieces and serve with the *salsa verde*.

Serves 4

NUTRIENT ANALYSIS PER SERVING 786 kJ – 194 cal – 16 g protein – 4 g carbohydrate – 0 g sugars – 12 g fat – 2 g saturated fat – 0 g fiber – 70 mg sodium

HEALTHY TIP As clams are low in fat, most of the fat in this recipe comes from the olive oil used in the *salsa verde*. Olive oil is a very good source of monounsaturated fatty acids. These are thought to help protect against coronary heart disease by increasing the ratio of "good" HDL cholesterol to "bad" LDL cholesterol.

Galician-style angler fish

rape Gallego This delicious fish dish from Galicia in northwestern Spain uses golden saffron and sweet almonds to flavor it. You could use any firm white fish fillets instead of the angler fish if you prefer. Serve with a mixed salad, or try the Leek Salad (*see page 75*) as an accompaniment.

INGREDIENTS *1 lb 10 oz angler fish fillet, skinned* ‖ *1 onion, very finely chopped* ‖ *olive oil, for drizzling* ‖ *15 whole blanched almonds, toasted and finely ground* ‖ *3 garlic cloves, crushed* ‖ *large pinch of saffron threads, crushed* ‖ *1 tablespoon finely chopped flat leaf parsley* ‖ *2–3 tablespoons water* ‖ *⅔ cup fresh or frozen peas* ‖ *salt and freshly ground black pepper*

ONE Cut the angler fish into 8 evenly sized pieces. Spread the onion out over the base of a medium-sized flameproof casserole and arrange the angler fish over the top. Season to taste with salt and pepper and drizzle over a little oil. Cover tightly and cook over a medium heat for 5–6 minutes. **TWO** Meanwhile, put the ground almonds, garlic, saffron, and parsley in a small bowl with the measurement water and blend together to make a smooth paste. **THREE** Spread the mixture over the top of the fish and add the peas. Re-cover and cook for an additional 4–5 minutes or until the fish is cooked through. Serve immediately.

Serves 4

NUTRIENT ANALYSIS PER SERVING 1048 kJ – 248 cal – 37 g protein – 10 g carbohydrate – 4 g sugars – 7 g fat – 1 g saturated fat – 6 g fiber – 40 mg sodium

HEALTHY TIP Angler fish is a very low-fat fish, so most of the small amount of fat in this recipe comes from the almonds and olive oil. Both of these are rich in beneficial monounsaturated fat. Onions and garlic may help to avert coronary heart disease by lowering the risk of blood clots forming.

Pickled mackerel *caballa en escabeche*

In this wonderfully simple recipe, mackerel fillets are left to marinate overnight in a herbed and spiced vinegar. They taste even better if eaten 2–3 days later (store in an airtight container in the refrigerator). You can use fresh sardine fillets instead of mackerel.

INGREDIENTS *1 lb 10 oz mackerel fillets* ‖ *4 tablespoons all-purpose flour* ‖ *1 tablespoon pimentón dulce (mild paprika)* ‖ *1 teaspoon sea salt* ‖ *2 tablespoons olive oil* ‖ *2 garlic cloves, finely chopped* ‖ *1 small red onion, cut into thin rings* ‖ *1 small carrot, cut into small dice* ‖ *4 tablespoons finely chopped flat leaf parsley* ‖ *1 teaspoon chopped oregano leaves* ‖ *1 bay leaf* ‖ *6 black peppercorns* ‖ *6 tablespoons white wine vinegar* ‖ *4 tablespoons water*

ONE Cut the mackerel fillets into large pieces. Put the flour on a plate with the *pimentón* and salt and mix together. Dust the fish pieces with the seasoned flour. **TWO** Heat the oil in a large, nonstick skillet, add the fish and cook for 1–2 minutes on each side. Remove from the pan with a slotted spoon and put in a shallow, non-reactive heatproof dish in a single layer. **THREE** Add the garlic, onion, and carrot to the pan with the parsley, oregano, bay leaf, and peppercorns. Pour in the vinegar and measurement water and bring to a boil. Remove from the heat and pour the mixture over the fish. **FOUR** Allow to cool, then cover and allow to marinate overnight in the refrigerator before serving.

Serves 4

NUTRIENT ANALYSIS PER SERVING 2412 kJ – 580 cal – 40 g protein – 19 g carbohydrate – 3 g sugars – 39 g fat – 7 g saturated fat – 2 g fiber – 760 mg sodium

HEALTHY TIP Mackerel is a particularly good source of omega-3 fat, which is believed to lower triglycerides (blood fats), reduce the risk of blood clotting, and protect against coronary heart disease.

Baked sardines
sardinas al horno Sardines are particularly valued by the Spanish, but they must be absolutely fresh and firm, not tired or limp. Ask your fish supplier to fillet the fish but keep them whole, so that they can be opened out like a book to season and then closed up again to cook and serve. Here, they are baked with a spiced tomato mixture and are equally good served at room temperature. Either way, serve with warm crusty bread.

INGREDIENTS *3 tablespoons olive oil* ‖ *2 onions, finely chopped* ‖ *4 garlic cloves, crushed* ‖ *1 red sweet pepper, cored, seeded, and finely chopped* ‖ *7 oz can chopped tomatoes* ‖ *1 teaspoon pimentón picante (hot paprika)* ‖ *large pinch of saffron threads* ‖ *½ teaspoon ground cumin* ‖ *1 bay leaf* ‖ *1 cinnamon stick* ‖ *3 tablespoons finely chopped flat leaf parsley, plus extra to garnish* ‖ *12 medium or 20–25 small fresh whole sardines, prepared (see page 14) and filleted but kept whole* ‖ *salt and freshly ground black pepper*

ONE Heat the oil in a large skillet, add the onions, garlic, and sweet pepper and cook over a low heat, stirring occasionally, for 10–15 minutes. **TWO** Add the tomatoes and their juice, *pimentón*, saffron, cumin, bay leaf, cinnamon stick, and parsley, season to taste with salt and pepper and cook, stirring occasionally, for an additional 8–10 minutes. **THREE** Gently open out the sardine fillets and lightly season with salt and pepper. Fold back into their original shape. Spread half the tomato mixture over the base of a medium-sized, shallow ovenproof dish or *cazuela* (*see page 13*). Arrange half the sardines on top in a single layer. Repeat with the remaining tomato mixture and sardines. **FOUR** Bake in a preheated oven, 400°F, for 15–20 minutes or until the fish is cooked through. Remove from the oven and serve immediately, garnished with a little finely chopped parsley.

Serves 4–6

NUTRIENT ANALYSIS PER SERVING 1544 kJ – 370 cal – 33 g protein – 10 g carbohydrate – 8 g sugars – 23 g fat – 5 g saturated fat – 2 g fiber – 203 mg sodium

HEALTHY TIP A fatty fish, sardines are a convenient source of polyunsaturated fatty acids. These are thought to be particularly important in the maintenance of "good" HDL cholesterol in the blood and the prevention of heart disease.

Stuffed baby squid *calamares rellenos* This dish of tender squid stuffed with

pine nuts and raisins from Majorca makes an easy and very tasty meal served with rustic bread and a crisp green salad. Alternatively, serve with Potatoes with Tomatoes (*see page 48*).

INGREDIENTS *1 lb 10 oz small or baby squid, prepared (see page 14)* ‖ *6 green onions, very finely chopped* ‖ *½ cup toasted pine nuts* ‖ *⅓ cup raisins* ‖ *2 small eggs, lightly beaten* ‖ *2 cups fresh white bread crumbs* ‖ *1 teaspoon ground cinnamon* ‖ *¾ cup white wine* ‖ *¾ cup store-bought or homemade Vegetable Stock (see page 16)* ‖ *large pinch of saffron threads* ‖ *olive oil, for drizzling* ‖ *salt and freshly ground black pepper*

ONE Finely chop about 4–5 tablespoonfuls of the squid tentacles and put in a bowl (the remainder can be used in a fish stew). **TWO** Add the green onions, pine nuts, raisins, eggs, and bread crumbs to the tentacles and mix together to form a relatively firm mixture. Add the cinnamon and season to taste with salt and pepper. **THREE** Stuff the squid body cavities with the mixture and arrange in a single layer in a large *cazuela (see page 13)* or large, shallow flameproof casserole. Pour over the wine and stock, sprinkle with the saffron, and drizzle with a little oil. **FOUR** Bring to a boil, then reduce the heat to low and simmer, uncovered, for 25–30 minutes, turning the squid over occasionally, until tender. Serve immediately.

Serves 4

NUTRIENT ANALYSIS PER SERVING 1730 kJ – 413 cal – 38 g protein – 24 g carbohydrate – 11 g sugars – 15 g fat – 2 g saturated fat – 2 g fiber – 526 mg sodium

HEALTHY TIP The addition of raisins, pine nuts, and eggs to the squid gives this dish a useful iron content. Pine nuts also contain lots of the antioxidant vitamin E, while raisins are a great source of potassium.

Broiled scallops *vieiras de Vigo*

This broiled scallop dish makes a perfect supper served with a mixed salad or the Red Onion and Orange Salad (*see page 71*), and crusty bread. If you don't want to prepare the scallops yourself, ask your fish supplier to do it for you and give you the shells.

INGREDIENTS *12 raw scallops, prepared (see page 14), 8 shells reserved* ‖ *1 garlic clove, very finely chopped* ‖ *1 tablespoon very finely chopped shallot* ‖ *2 tablespoons very finely chopped tomato* ‖ *¼ teaspoon finely grated lemon zest* ‖ *1 tablespoon lemon juice* ‖ *2 tablespoons very finely chopped flat leaf parsley* ‖ *3 tablespoons fresh white bread crumbs* ‖ *olive oil, for drizzling* ‖ *salt and freshly ground black pepper*

ONE Roughly chop the scallops and put in a bowl. Add the garlic, shallot, tomato, lemon zest and juice, and parsley. Season to taste with salt and pepper and mix well to combine. **TWO** Divide the scallop mixture between the scallop shells and sprinkle with the bread crumbs. Drizzle with a little oil. **THREE** Cook under a preheated medium-high broiler for 6–8 minutes or until lightly golden and the scallops are just cooked through. Serve immediately.

Serves 4

NUTRIENT ANALYSIS PER SERVING 580 kJ – 137 cal – 19 g protein – 10 g carbohydrate – 1 g sugars – 3 g fat – 1 g saturated fat – 1 g fiber – 200 mg sodium

HEALTHY TIP Scallops contain useful amounts of trace minerals such as copper and selenium, as well as small amounts of B vitamins. They are also low in fat. In general, low-fat fish contain less vitamins and minerals than the fatty fish, but all low-fat fish make a very healthy source of protein.

Clams in white wine

almejas en vino The small creamy, orange-fleshed clams from Spain used in this recipe are also known as *almendras de mar* (sea almonds) and are sweet and delicate in flavor. Use any other fresh clams if you can't get hold of this variety. Serve with crusty bread to mop up the juices.

INGREDIENTS *2–3 tablespoons olive oil* ‖ *2 garlic cloves, crushed* ‖ *1 small dried chili, crushed* ‖ *1 cup sweet sherry* ‖ *4 tablespoons finely chopped flat leaf parsley* ‖ *2 lb live clams, prepared* (see page 14)

ONE Heat the oil in a large saucepan, add the garlic and chili and cook over a medium heat, stirring, for 30–40 seconds. Add the sherry and parsley and bring to a boil. **TWO** Add the drained clams to the pan, cover, and cook over a high heat, shaking the pan vigorously several times, for 4–5 minutes or until all the clams have opened (discard any of them that remain closed). **THREE** Ladle the clams into warmed bowls and serve immediately.

Serves 4

NUTRIENT ANALYSIS PER SERVING 1307 kJ – 322 cal – 32 g protein – 11 g carbohydrate – 4 g sugars – 8 g fat – 1 g saturated fat – 0 g fiber – 150 mg sodium

HEALTHY TIP This recipe contains a relatively large amount of parsley, which is nutritious for its content of vitamin C. Parsley is often used simply as a garnish, which means that we usually do not eat enough for it to make a major contribution to our regular vitamin C intake.

Baked crabs Basque style

txangurro al horno Txangurro is the Basque name for the big spider or spiny crabs found in the Bay of Biscay. This recipe uses regular crabs, available from any quality fish supplier. If you can't find whole crabs, use about 13 oz cooked crabmeat and bake in individual ovenproof dishes.

INGREDIENTS *4 whole freshly cooked crabs* ‖ *2 tablespoons olive oil, plus extra for drizzling* ‖ *2 onions, finely chopped* ‖ *2 garlic cloves, finely chopped* ‖ *2 ripe tomatoes, skinned, seeded, and finely chopped* ‖ *4 tablespoons chopped flat leaf parsley, plus extra to garnish* ‖ *6 tablespoons dry white wine* ‖ *6 tablespoons store-bought or homemade Fish or Vegetable Stock (see pages 16–17)* ‖ *1 teaspoon pimentón dulce (mild paprika)* ‖ *2 tablespoons fresh white bread crumbs* ‖ *salt and freshly ground black pepper*

ONE Pick out all the meat from the cooked crabs and set aside. Wash the crab shells, pat them dry and set them aside on a baking sheet. **TWO** Heat the oil in a large, nonstick skillet, add the onions and garlic and cook over a low heat, stirring occasionally, for 10–12 minutes until the onions are very soft. **THREE** Add the tomatoes and cook over a medium heat, stirring frequently, for 10 minutes. Add the parsley, wine, and stock and season to taste with salt and pepper. Cook for 3–4 minutes, then add the *pimentón* and crabmeat. Cook, stirring, for 3–4 minutes. **FOUR** Pack the mixture into the crab shells, sprinkle over the bread crumbs and drizzle with oil. Bake in a preheated oven, 400°F, for 8–10 minutes or until the tops are just lightly browned. Serve immediately, garnished with chopped parsley.

Serves 4

NUTRIENT ANALYSIS PER SERVING 1360 kJ – 325 cal – 32 g protein – 12 g carbohydrate – 6 g sugars – 15 g fat – 2 g saturated fat – 2 g fiber – 600 mg sodium

HEALTHY TIP Crab is an excellent low-fat source of protein. It also contains small amounts of B vitamins and a number of trace minerals, such as copper, zinc, and selenium.

Traditional fish and potato stew

marmita-kua This robust one-pot fish stew from the Basque region gets its name from the utensil that it is traditionally cooked in—a *marmita*. You can use any firm fresh fish in place of the tuna.

INGREDIENTS *1 lb 10 oz tuna fillets, cut into large bite-size pieces* ‖ *4 tablespoons olive oil* ‖ *2 red onions, halved and thinly sliced* ‖ *4 garlic cloves, thinly sliced* ‖ *3 ripe tomatoes, skinned, seeded, and chopped* ‖ *2 bay leaves* ‖ *1 red sweet pepper, cored, seeded, and diced* ‖ *1 tablespoon pimentón dulce (mild paprika)* ‖ *1¼ lb potatoes, peeled and cut into large bite-size pieces* ‖ *salt and freshly ground black pepper*

TO GARNISH *chopped flat leaf parsley* ‖ *capers*

ONE Arrange the tuna in a shallow bowl in a single layer and season to taste with salt and pepper. Cover and set aside. **TWO** Heat the oil in a medium-sized saucepan, add the onions and garlic and cook over a medium heat, stirring frequently, for 8–10 minutes until soft. **THREE** Add the tomatoes, bay leaves, sweet pepper, *pimentón*, and potatoes and stir to mix well. Add enough water to just cover all the ingredients and bring to a boil. Reduce the heat and simmer gently for 25–30 minutes or until the potatoes are tender. **FOUR** Add the fish, return to a boil and cook for 4–5 minutes. **FIVE** Taste and adjust the seasoning if necessary, then serve ladled into warmed shallow bowls, garnished with chopped parsley and capers.

Serves 4

NUTRIENT ANALYSIS PER SERVING 2299 kJ – 547 cal – 53 g protein – 39 g carbohydrate – 11 g sugars – 21 g fat – 4 g saturated fat – 6 g fiber – 119 mg sodium

HEALTHY TIP Tuna is a low-fat fish and an excellent source of protein. Like many fish, it contains useful amounts of selenium, which is necessary for a healthy thyroid. The combination of tuna with potatoes, tomatoes, and onions makes this a particularly nutritious dish.

Mixed fish stew

zarzuela The name *zarzuela* actually means a light opera in Spain. But in this context it signifies a sublime mixture of fresh fish and shellfish, cooked in white wine. You can vary the ingredients and proportions to whatever combination you desire.

INGREDIENTS *2 tablespoons olive oil* ‖ *12 raw jumbo shrimp in their shells* ‖ *1 onion, finely chopped* ‖ *4 garlic cloves, crushed* ‖ *2 ripe tomatoes, chopped* ‖ *1 bay leaf* ‖ *large pinch of saffron threads* ‖ *1 teaspoon pimentón dulce (mild paprika)* ‖ *1 dried red chili* ‖ *1 cup dry white wine* ‖ *13 oz firm white fish fillets, such as cod or halibut, cut into bite-size pieces* ‖ *4 small squid, prepared (see page 14) and sliced* ‖ *6 live mussels, prepared (see page 14)* ‖ *1 tablespoon ground almonds* ‖ *3 tablespoons finely chopped flat leaf parsley, plus extra whole leaves to garnish* ‖ *salt and freshly ground black pepper*

ONE Heat the oil in a large, shallow flameproof casserole, add the whole shrimp and cook over a high heat until they turn pink. Remove with a slotted spoon to a plate and set aside. Add the onion and half the garlic and cook over a low heat, stirring occasionally, for 10 minutes until the onion is soft. **TWO** Add the tomatoes, bay leaf, saffron, *pimentón*, chili, and wine and bring to a boil. Add the fish and squid and cook, stirring occasionally, for 5 minutes, then add the mussels and cook, stirring occasionally, for 4–5 minutes or until they have all opened (discard any that remain closed). **THREE** Mix the ground almonds with the remaining garlic and the parsley and stir into the casserole. Season to taste with salt and pepper and return the shrimp with any juices that have accumulated to the casserole. Stir to mix well, then ladle into warmed shallow soup plates and serve immediately, garnished with a few parsley leaves.

Serves 4–6

NUTRIENT ANALYSIS PER SERVING 1310 kJ – 313 cal – 40 g protein – 6 g carbohydrate – 4 g sugars – 10 g fat – 1 g saturated fat – 2 g fiber – 340 mg sodium

HEALTHY TIP A hearty fish stew that is low in fat and high in protein. Tomatoes contain the antioxidant lycopene, which studies suggest may have a role in preventing cancer by suppressing the growth of tumors and inactivating carcinogens.

Desserts

Peaches in wine *melocotones en vino*

It is natural that, with such an abundance throughout Spain, fruit is often served to conclude a meal. Here, fragrant ripe peaches are enlivened with cinnamon-spiced red wine. This recipe works equally well with fresh pears.

INGREDIENTS *4 ripe peaches* ‖ *1½ cups dry red wine* ‖ *⅓ cup golden superfine sugar* ‖ *4 thin slices of lemon, seeds removed* ‖ *1 cinnamon stick, plus extra pieces to garnish* ‖ *1½ cups water* ‖ *crème fraîche or sour cream, to serve*

ONE Bring a large saucepan of water to a boil. Add the peaches and leave for 30 seconds. Drain and plunge into cold water, then peel away the skins. **TWO** Put the peaches in a saucepan large enough to hold them in a single layer and add the wine, sugar, lemon slices, cinnamon, and measurement water. Bring to a simmer, cover, and cook for 12–15 minutes or until tender. **THREE** Remove the peaches with a slotted spoon and transfer to a shallow heatproof serving dish. Boil the remaining liquid in the saucepan over a high heat for 6–8 minutes or until reduced and syrupy. Remove from the heat and pour over the peaches. **FOUR** Leave to cool, then cover, and chill in the refrigerator for 2 hours. Serve the peaches in individual bowls or on plates with the syrup drizzled over and a dollop of crème fraîche or sour cream. Garnish each serving with a piece of cinnamon stick.

Serves 4

NUTRIENT ANALYSIS PER SERVING 720 kJ – 170 cal – 1 g protein – 28 g carbohydrate – 28 g sugars – 0 g fat – 0 g saturated fat – 3 g fiber – 10 mg sodium

HEALTHY TIP Peaches contain useful amounts of vitamin C and the vitamin B group. Like many yellow-fleshed fruits and vegetables, they also contain carotene, the precursor to vitamin A. All these vitamins will help maintain a healthy immune system, while carotene and vitamin C are important antioxidants, which are thought to have a role in the prevention of cancer.

Stuffed figs

higos rellenos Summertime in Spain sees a glut of this luscious fruit, which has over 60 varieties. As they cannot all be eaten fresh, many are dried, and this recipe makes excellent use of them, poached in honey- and cinnamon-flavored sherry.

INGREDIENTS ⅔ *cup clear honey* ‖ *6 tablespoons sweet, dark sherry, such as Pedro Ximenez* ‖ *1 teaspoon ground cinnamon* ‖ *12 large dried figs* ‖ *1¼ cups water* ‖ *12 whole blanched almonds* ‖ *low-fat plain yogurt or half-fat crème fraîche, to serve*

ONE Put the honey, sherry, cinnamon, figs, and measurement water in a saucepan over a medium-high heat and bring to a boil. Reduce the heat and simmer gently for 10–12 minutes. Remove from the heat and allow to stand, covered, for 3–4 hours. **TWO** Remove the figs from the pan with a slotted spoon, reserving the liquid. Bring the liquid to a boil over a high heat and boil for 4–5 minutes until thick and syrupy. Remove from the heat and set aside. **THREE** Using a small, sharp knife, make a small slit in the top of each fig and stuff it with an almond. Serve the figs drizzled with the warm syrup, with a dollop of yogurt or crème fraîche.

Serves 4

NUTRIENT ANALYSIS PER SERVING 1366 kJ – 322 cal – 4 g protein – 64 g carbohydrate – 64 g sugars – 5 g fat – 0 g saturated fat – 9 g fiber – 47 mg sodium

HEALTHY TIP Dried figs are a good source of dietary fiber, essential in helping the bowels work well and preventing constipation. Figs also contain useful amounts of calcium and magnesium, vital for the maintenance of bone tissue.

Almond and lemon cake *tarta de almendras y limón*

This delightfully scented cake, flavored with almonds and lemons, does not use any flour. It is particularly delicious served with a dollop of plain yogurt and fresh berries.

INGREDIENTS *4 eggs* ‖ *¾ cup golden superfine sugar* ‖ *finely grated zest of 1 lemon* ‖ *juice of 1 lemon* ‖ *3½ cups ground almonds* ‖ *confectioners' sugar, for dusting*

ONE Grease an 8 inch square removable-bottomed cake tin and line the base with parchment paper or waxed paper. **TWO** Beat the eggs with an electric beater in a large bowl until pale and frothy. Gradually add the superfine sugar and continue beating until pale and stiff. **THREE** Using a metal spoon, gently fold in the lemon zest and juice and the ground almonds until well combined. **FOUR** Spoon the cake mixture into the prepared tin and bake in a preheated oven, 375°F, for 35–40 minutes or until browned and firm to touch, and a skewer inserted into the center comes out clean. **FIVE** Transfer to a wire rack and allow to cool for 10 minutes before turning out. Remove and discard the lining paper. Dust with confectioners' sugar before serving, cut into squares.

Serves 6

NUTRIENT ANALYSIS PER SERVING 2406 kJ – 577 cal – 19 g protein – 35 g carbohydrate – 34 g sugars – 41 g fat – 4 g saturated fat – 9 g fiber – 60 mg sodium

HEALTHY TIP The almonds used in this cake make it quite high in dietary fiber. Eggs provide iron, as well as vitamins A and D. Most of our vitamin D is obtained by the action of daylight on skin, but eggs are one of the comparatively few dietary sources of the vitamin.

Cinnamon ice cream

helado de canela In Spain, ice cream is rarely served at home, but is a treat to be frequently enjoyed at pavement cafés and in restaurants. This cinnamon-flavored ice cream is a particular summertime favorite, and this version is made with vanilla-flavored yogurt for a guilt-free indulgence.

INGREDIENTS *3 cups vanilla-flavored yogurt ‖ 2 tablespoons ground cinnamon ‖ 1 teaspoon finely grated lemon zest ‖ 4 tablespoons confectioners' sugar ‖ sweet cookies, to serve (optional)*

ONE Mix all the ingredients together in a large bowl until well combined. Transfer the mixture to an ice-cream machine and churn until frozen, following the manufacturer's instructions. Transfer to a shallow freezerproof container and freeze until ready to use. **TWO** Alternatively, transfer to a shallow freezerproof container and freeze for 3–4 hours or until almost solid. Beat well with an electric beater or transfer to a blender or food processor and blend until smooth, then return to the freezer. **THREE** Beat or blend in the same way after every 2 hours of freezing to break down all the ice crystals until the ice cream is smooth, then freeze again until solid. **FOUR** Transfer the ice cream to the refrigerator 20 minutes before serving. Scoop into chilled dessert glasses and serve with sweet cookies, if desired.

Serves 4

NUTRIENT ANALYSIS PER SERVING 1056 kJ – 248 cal – 7 g protein – 55 g carbohydrate – 55 g sugars – 2 g fat – 1 g saturated fat – 0 g fiber – 120 mg sodium

HEALTHY TIP The yogurt used for this low-fat ice cream is an excellent source of calcium, magnesium, and phosphorus. Calcium is essential for the maintenance of healthy bones, which become a particular health worry for women after the menopause.

Blood orange popsicles *helado de naranja sanguina*

The south coast of Valencia is known as the Costa del Azahar (coast of the orange blossom) and sailors are reputed to have been able to smell the fragrance of the native fruit up to ten nautical miles away. These popsicles made with pure blood orange juice are so simple to prepare and really refreshing on a hot summer's day. Alternatively, you can use the juice of any ripe, fragrant oranges.

INGREDIENTS *2 cups freshly squeezed blood orange juice* ‖ *2 tablespoons confectioners' sugar*

ONE Mix the blood orange juice and sugar together in a large pitcher. **TWO** Pour the juice mixture into 4 popsicle molds and freeze for 3–4 hours or until solid. **THREE** When ready to serve, dip the popsicle molds in hot water for 20–30 seconds, then pop the popsicles out. Serve immediately.

Serves 4

NUTRIENT ANALYSIS PER SERVING 300 kJ – 70 cal – 1 g protein – 18 g carbohydrate – 18 g sugars – 0 g fat – 0 g saturated fat – 0 g fiber – 3 mg sodium

HEALTHY TIP Orange juice is a particularly good source of vitamin C, an essential antioxidant, and vital for the protection and maintenance of body tissue. Oranges are also high in carotenes, which are thought to have an important role in protecting against cancer.

Almond milk _horchata_

This sumptuously creamy almond drink is to be found all over juice bars and ice-cream parlors in Spain. It is also available in cartons from grocery stores and supermarkets. Use the finest-quality Spanish almonds for this refreshing and nutritious drink.

INGREDIENTS _2¼ cups whole blanched almonds_ ‖ _6 cups water_ ‖ _2 tablespoons golden superfine sugar_ ‖ _pinch of ground cinnamon_ ‖ _crushed ice, to serve_

ONE Put the almonds in a food processor with 1¾ cups of the measurement water and process until as smooth as possible. **TWO** Transfer to a bowl with the remaining water and stir well. Cover and leave to infuse overnight in the refrigerator. **THREE** Strain the liquid through very fine cheese-cloth into a saucepan and add the sugar and cinnamon. Bring the mixture to a boil, then remove from the heat and allow to cool. Transfer to a pitcher or bowl, cover, and chill in the refrigerator for 3–4 hours. **FOUR** When ready to serve, fill 4 tall glasses with crushed ice, pour the almond milk over and serve immediately.

Serves 4

NUTRIENT ANALYSIS PER SERVING 1118 kJ – 269 cal – 8 g protein – 13 g carbohydrate – 12 g sugars – 21 g fat – 2 g saturated fat – 0 g fiber – 11 mg sodium

HEALTHY TIP Almonds, like most nuts, are a great way of consuming vitamin E, which is a valuable antioxidant. They also contain useful amounts of the B vitamins and are quite a good source of calcium, magnesium, and phosphorus.

Spanish custard creams

natillas These creamy cinnamon-flavored custards are perfect to follow a spicy main course. You can add finely grated orange or lemon zest to the mixture for added flavor if you desire.

INGREDIENTS *3 cups lowfat milk* ‖ *1 cinnamon stick* ‖ *6 egg yolks* ‖ *⅔ cup golden superfine sugar* ‖ *2 teaspoons cornstarch* ‖ *ground cinnamon, for dusting* ‖ *sweet cookies, to serve (optional)*

ONE Bring all but 3 tablespoons of the milk and cinnamon stick to a boil in a saucepan over a medium heat. Meanwhile, beat the egg yolks and sugar with an electric beater in a large bowl until light and frothy. **TWO** Blend the cornstarch with the remaining milk in a cup, then add to the egg yolk mixture. Beat well to combine. **THREE** When the milk comes to a boil, remove from the heat and remove the cinnamon stick. Gradually add the egg mixture, stirring constantly, and then return the pan to a very low heat and cook, stirring constantly, until the custard thickens. Remove from the heat and allow to cool before spooning into individual bowls or dessert glasses. **FOUR** Cover and chill for 2–3 hours or overnight. Lightly dust with ground cinnamon before serving, accompanied by sweet cookies, if you desire.

Serves 4

NUTRIENT ANALYSIS PER SERVING 1412 kJ – 334 cal – 11 g protein – 51 g carbohydrate – 49 g sugars – 11 g fat – 4 g saturated fat – 0 g fiber – 46 mg sodium

HEALTHY TIP These custards are very rich in calcium and they also contain egg yolks, high in vitamin D. This vitamin plays a vital role in maintaining bone calcium levels. A diet rich in vitamin D is essential for the house-bound, or anyone who is not able to expose their skin to sunlight.

Sparkling peach sangria *sangría de melocotón* This sparkling sangria uses cava, Spanish sparkling white wine, and sliced peaches. Try to use the ripest, sweetest peaches you can find for this special-occasion drink.

INGREDIENTS *4 ripe peaches, skinned (see page 146), pitted, and sliced* ‖ *2 tablespoons golden superfine sugar* ‖ *5 tablespoons peach-flavored liqueur* ‖ *1 small lemon, halved and thinly sliced* ‖ *¾ cup peach juice* ‖ *3 cups chilled cava or any other sparkling dry white wine* ‖ *ice cubes or crushed ice, to serve*

ONE Put the peaches, sugar, liqueur, lemon slices, and peach juice in a bowl. Cover and chill overnight in the refrigerator. **TWO** When ready to serve, fill 6 tall, chilled glasses with ice. Transfer the peach mixture to a large pitcher or bowl. Pour over the cava or other sparkling white wine, stir and pour into the prepared glasses, spooning some of the sliced fruit into each one. Serve immediately.

Serves 6

NUTRIENT ANALYSIS PER SERVING 1169 kJ – 277 cal – 2 g protein – 30 g carbohydrate – 30 g sugars – 0 g fat – 0 g saturated fat – 3 g fiber – 16 mg sodium

HEALTHY TIP The peach juice in this drink contains vitamins B and C, as well as carotene, the precursor to vitamin A. Bear in mind that the alcohol in sparkling wine is absorbed into the bloodstream more quickly than that in still wine—enjoy it slowly!

Index

Acknowledgments

EXECUTIVE EDITOR Nicky Hill

EDITOR Fiona Robertson

ART DIRECTOR Geoff Fennell

PHOTOGRAPHY Jason Lowe /© Octopus Publishing Group Ltd

FOOD STYLIST Sunil Vijayakar

PROP STYLIST Liz Hippisley

SENIOR PRODUCTION CONTROLLER Manjit Sihra